"Rick Mattson's apologetic i   :t and easy
to use. These images are   –they are
thoughtful, subtle, flexible   .nd they are
clearly born out of the clarifying furnace of Rick's real-life relationships
and ministry. For decades Rick has invested in the lives of seekers and
skeptics, and *Faith Is Like Skydiving* is not just a thoughtful, practical re-
flection on all he's learned—it's a gift to today's church."

Don Everts, author of *Jesus with Dirty Feet, Go and Do* and *I Once Was Lost* (with
Doug Schaupp)

"*Faith Is Like Skydiving* is a wonderfully practical how-to guide for aspiring
apologists. Mattson covers a nice range of topics, offering creative analogies by which to communicate thoughtful answers to tough questions.
Highly recommended!"

Paul Rhodes Eddy, professor of biblical and theological studies, Bethel University

"Want to share about Jesus with skeptics with a tone of grace and truth?
Read and practice this book. Rick knows his stuff. Reading this book is
like going with Rick on a road trip to campus and getting trained by him
on how to talk to atheists about faith. Rick's style is conversational,
winsome, practical and confident. This book is full of tried-and-true material that will help you relax and communicate well. He simplifies the
complex philosophical topics. He gives great pointers for you to practice.
There is something for everyone in these pages."

Doug Schaupp, coauthor of *I Once Was Lost*, associate national director of
evangelism for InterVarsity Christian Fellowship

"Apologists sometimes deserve their reputation for focusing exclusively on
data, evidence or arguments. These are essential to faith. But apologetics
is both science and art. To the proper emphasis on reasons for faith—the
science—we rightly add a stress on finding ways to apply spiritual truth
in real life. This is about genuine communication in the context of authentic relationships—the art. To bring apologetics into the real world,
you must use your imagination. Rick Mattson is a master of imagination.
As you mull over his images, I hope you'll gain new insights. I bet you'll
think of your own analogies. And best of all, I believe you'll feel empowered to enjoy apologetic dialogues in whole new ways."

David K. Clark, vice president and dean, Bethel Seminary, author,
Dialogical Apologetics

"*Faith Is Like Skydiving* offers an inspiring guide to engaging people with real and relevant questions. This short work reads like a field book for talking with everyday people about everyday questions and objections to faith. Rick's down-to-earth and transparent writing is matched by the many encounters with real people he's been able to engage with where they are at. This book should be on every vocational Christian worker's short, go-to list for resources on engaging people in the art of apologetics. This book should also be basic reading for everyday Christians who care about the people around them, who often have real questions and are open to real answers."

R. York Moore, national evangelist, InterVarsity Christian Fellowship USA, author of *Growing Your Faith by Giving It Away* and *Making All Things New*

FAITH IS LIKE SKYDIVING

AND OTHER MEMORABLE IMAGES FOR DIALOGUE WITH SEEKERS AND SKEPTICS

RICK MATTSON

IVP Books

An imprint of InterVarsity Press
Downers Grove, Illinois

InterVarsity Press
P.O. Box 1400, Downers Grove, IL 60515-1426
World Wide Web: www.ivpress.com
Email: email@ivpress.com

InterVarsity Press® is the book-publishing division of InterVarsity Christian Fellowship/USA®, a movement of students and faculty active on campus at hundreds of universities, colleges and schools of nursing in the United States of America, and a member movement of the International Fellowship of Evangelical Students. For information about local and regional activities, write Public Relations Dept., InterVarsity Christian Fellowship/USA, 6400 Schroeder Rd., P.O. Box 7895, Madison, WI 53707-7895, or visit the IVCF website at www.intervarsity.org.

All Scripture quotations, unless otherwise indicated, are taken from THE HOLY BIBLE, NEW INTERNATIONAL VERSION®, NIV® Copyright © 1973, 1978, 1984, 2011 by Biblica, Inc.™ Used by permission. All rights reserved worldwide.

While all stories in this book are true, some names and identifying information in this book have been changed to protect the privacy of the individuals involved.

Cover design: Cindy Kiple
Interior design: Beth Hagenberg
Images: skydivers: © 4x6/iStockphoto
     parachuting: © filo/iStockphoto

ISBN 978-0-8308-4411-1 (print)
ISBN 978-0-8308-7967-0 (digital)

Printed in the United States of America ∞

Library of Congress Cataloging-in-Publication Data
A catalog record for this book is available from the Library of Congress.

P	17	16	15	14	13	12	11	10	9	8	7	6	5	4	3	2	1
Y	28	27	26	25	24	23	22	21	20	19	18	17	16	15	14		

CONTENTS

Acknowledgments.   7

Introduction.   9

PART ONE: MAKING YOUR CASE

1 Faith Is Like Skydiving   17
   Look Before You Leap!

2 Play Your Whole Orchestra   28
   The Cumulative Case for Faith

3 How the World Came to Be   36
   The Grand Designer

4 The World Is Like a Royal Flush   46
   A Case for the Design of the Universe

PART TWO: RESPONDING TO TOUGH QUESTIONS

5 Jesus as the Son of God   61
   A Massive Conspiracy?

6 The Telephone Game   76
   Why the Bible Is Not Full of Errors

7 Broken World   83
   And Other Images for the Problem of Suffering and Evil

8 Christians Behaving Badly   97
   Don't Blame the Hammer

9 Religions Are Like Books   110
And Other Images for Discussing Religious Pluralism

10 Can Those Who've Never Heard of
Jesus Be Saved?   122
The Homeless Person Analogy

11 Hell Is Like an Empty Pub.   133

PART THREE: SCIENCE AND FAITH

12 Elephant Traps.   145
And Other Images for Science and Faith

13 Miracles Are Like a Hole in One   159

PART FOUR: HOW-TO'S

14 How to Talk with Skeptics.   171
An Introduction

15 How to Talk with Modern Skeptics
Who Believe in God   179

16 How to Talk with Modern Atheists   185

17 How to Talk with Postmodern
Seekers and Skeptics.   199

Epilogue   213
A Word of Encouragement

Notes   215

Index   229

ACKNOWLEDGMENTS

To my many critical readers and ministry supporters for encouraging me in this project, thank you. Your imprint is on every page.

To the InterVarsity staff and student leaders on the front lines who are my true teammates in my travels, thank you so much. Before it was written, this book "took place" in your student unions, dorm lounges and coffee shops.

To my wonderful wife, Sharon, who read every word of the manuscript (twice!). I dedicate this book to you, my dear.

INTRODUCTION

I DON'T GET IT, RICK. Where is God in all this? I thought God actually cared about me and could do something useful! Maybe I haven't been the most faithful Christian or whatever, but why would he let all this [bleep] happen to me? And it's not just me! The whole world is [bleep]!" Daniel shook his head and clenched a fist. "I'm having a hard time believing. I want to believe in God. But where is he? Why doesn't he do something about this mess I'm in?"

We were sitting in a Wendy's in St. Paul, Minnesota. Daniel had been showing interest in Christianity of late, the result of some hard times in his life. Years ago he'd attended church for a while, but he never really dove in all the way, never took the step of becoming a true follower of Christ.

The big mistake was marrying Lori. Gorgeous Lori. They were only nineteen, and she'd gotten him off track. His fledgling spiritual life was put on hold. A baby came along and everything was great for a couple of years, but then he began having suspicions about Lori. Thursday nights she went out with the girls, and he wanted to trust her. But something wasn't right about the details.

She'd been lying. And now she was gone.

Here at Wendy's, over a number one combo and a Frosty, I was on the spot. Daniel was asking me for answers. Being in the ministry, I was supposed to be a pro at this stuff. Only one problem. I wasn't prepared. I had a tendency to overestimate my ability to improvise my way through these interactions. Here's how I responded to Daniel:

First, there was a minute or two of silence as I pondered what to say. Maybe not the worst thing in the world. You want to give a thoughtful reply, right? Show the other person that their questions are important. Actually, my mind was racing. I tried to remember the verse in 1 Peter or Romans about God letting his children go through hard times, but I couldn't come up with it. Rats.

I shifted gears and thought about the classic "problem of evil" and then C. S. Lewis's character Screwtape from *The Screwtape Letters*, which reminded me of the book *Mere Christianity* and how much it meant to my own conversion to Christ. Yeah, there was an idea! I could ask Daniel to read that book and we could meet once a week and talk about it! Wait, that was cold. This man was hurting and here I was planning out his reading curriculum.

Meanwhile, Daniel was giving me that "Well, are you going to answer the question, Mr. Christian? While we're still young?" look. So I meandered verbally with a few half-baked Bible references, and then I told a story about my second cousin who was dumped by his girlfriend. And I couldn't resist a mention of Screwtape and the devil's tactics against humanity. But hey, in my twenty-minute response to Daniel at least I said everything in a caring tone of voice and occasionally mentioned that I was "truly sorry for your pain."

Not my finest moment. A hurting person—a seeker of God— came to me with significant questions, and I stunk up the room with abstract ramblings. What I really needed was something concrete and concise, something memorable for Daniel that would make a difference in his life. Actually, something memorable for me as well, because I was coming up with nothing on the fly.

Maybe you've found yourself in the same boat. An opportunity presents itself for you to say something on behalf of God or the Bible, and you get stuck. Either you draw a blank or you ramble. Some of the opportunities, of course, are not in friendly situations. You probably know some folks who are antagonistic to Christianity, and they don't merely ask innocent questions; they come in with guns blazing.

Like Aunt Josephine.

I was spending Thanksgiving at Bill's house in Florida, away from my family in Minnesota, this particular year. Twenty or so of Bill's relatives were there, and I was going along great, making new friends and finding my niche in this nice family. Then everything went sideways. Politics. Little conversations around the table broke up to focus on two loud voices. This was the George Bush era, never mind which one, and the two loud voices led the whole crew into some Republican-bashing that somehow turned into church-bashing. Gosh, I never saw any of this coming.

Everyone knew I was in the ministry, including Aunt Josephine. No matter. She took the floor and spoke her mind in no uncertain terms, hitting on the Crusades and abortion and gay rights and TV preachers and Christian hypocrisy. At the ten-minute mark I knew I needed to say something. Unfortunately, in the heat of the moment, I felt panicky and intimidated. My face was getting hot, my hands shaky. I'm the philosophical type, so when I finally got to speak, with twenty pairs of eyes staring at me, I threw out something about Christianity being "ontologically true."

Yep, that was my best material. You can guess the rest. I didn't go down in flames, more like a whimper as a barrage of voices interrupted, then buried me.

Again, that's me unprepared. I want to be all organic and relational and, of course, never "prepackaged" or slick in my communication of Christian truth. I don't want to come across as a salesman of the gospel. Great. Those are fine motives, right? So my brilliant solution: Don't have a plan at all. Just wing it, then call that "reliance on the Holy Spirit."

THE PURPOSE OF THIS BOOK

My goal is to help you get out of the trap of being unprepared for the Daniels and Josephines in your life—seekers and skeptics with questions and objections. I want to provide you with a series of concrete, concise analogies that are easy to remember and that you can lay down in conversations without even thinking about it too hard. Skydiving, a royal flush, a massive conspiracy, the telephone game, an empty pub, elephant traps and many others: these images can serve as your "go-to" cards in a variety of situations. No more blanking out; no more rambling. Your confidence will increase. And you'll be able to spend your talk time with seekers and skeptics really praying and relying on the Holy Sprit instead of scrambling to ad lib your points.

At the end of the book I talk about how to get into these conversations in the first place and how your approaches to postmodern and modern people might differ. Plus there's a chapter dedicated to helping you converse with atheists—a community close to my heart.

INTENDED AUDIENCE

Who should read *Faith Is Like Skydiving*?

- Ordinary Christians who want to improve their conversational skills, especially their ability to address hard questions. No formal theological training is necessary. I've tried to make the apologetic material accessible for thoughtful laypersons.

- Ministry professionals who already have training and skills in outreach but who need to organize their thoughts around some concrete, concise images—and train others to do the same.

- Seekers and skeptics who want to learn more about the case for Christianity in a nontechnical format. Hopefully the images will enable you to understand why Christians think the way they do and perhaps help you move closer to God.

HAD I BEEN PREPARED . . .

Let's return to Daniel, the seeker of God, and Josephine, the angry skeptic. Instead of rambling or panicking, what could I have said in each situation that would have been relevant, crisp and memorable? That might have made a lasting impression and perhaps extended the conversation? Perhaps this:

> Daniel, I know this is really tough for you. Could I tell you a story? It takes about five minutes, and it's called the Big Story. At the heart of the story is an image I hope you'll remember: a broken world . . . (See chapter seven to learn more.)
>
> Josephine, you're right. Many times Christians have brought harm to others, and I want to acknowledge that. But there's an analogy about a hammer I'd like to share with you that brings out a couple of important nuances in this issue . . . (See chapter eight to learn more.)

FIELD-TESTED

You may wonder where all this material came from. The short answer: from a thousand conversations in my job as a traveling apologist for InterVarsity. My friends tease me that I'm out "apologizing for God." Actually, an apologist is someone who makes a case for Christian faith—a "lawyer" for Christianity, one might say. That means I hang out with a ton of students and faculty at colleges and universities around the country, the testing ground for the images and illustrations I'm offering here. And when I'm home I work for InterVarsity at Macalester College in St. Paul, Minnesota, another fabulously fertile ground for God talk with students from around the world.

As I've moved from being unprepared to prepared in conversations, it's made a huge difference. I feel more relaxed and confident in tight situations that paralyzed me before. The same will happen for you if you learn to use the analogies found in this book. Apologetic conversation (dialogue about tough questions) may still feel a little scary at times—like jumping out of an airplane! But at least now you'll have prepared yourself by packing a parachute.

PART ONE
MAKING YOUR CASE

1

FAITH IS LIKE SKYDIVING

Look Before You Leap!

WHEN EMILY ENTERED THE ROOM, she caught my eye but glanced away quickly, parking her lunch tray in the back of the room as she sat down. I was giving a noon-hour presentation titled "Faith, Evidence and Proof" at a private college in the Midwest. A dozen students and myself were jammed into tight quarters around an oblong table in a conference room off the dining center. Before long the conversation was sizzling, and Emily had no place to hide.

I called on her. She looked at me warily. She seemed conflicted—interested in the topic but, then again, maybe not wanting to be there at all. "I don't know if I could believe in God without some sort of proof," she said quietly.

"What kind of proof?" I asked. She shrugged. Her body language had me confused—it was a mix of "Don't call on me again; I don't want to talk" and a pleading manner, as if to say, "I want to be part of this community. I want to have my own faith, but I just can't right now. Yet here I am, searching . . ."

As it turned out, I would see Emily several times that week as I gave a series of outreach talks at her campus. And I learned that her faith struggles played out on two stages: emotional and intellectual.

Let's start with the emotional.

That's how I first came to faith. As a young musician touring the country with our family band ("The Mattsons"), I felt secure and important. But upon returning home at age nineteen, the bright lights were absent, my girlfriend had dumped me and I was truly a lost soul. Friends from high school shared Christ with me, and after several months of resistance I realized I needed whatever they had, whatever was making them overflow with vibrant joy and love—all of which contrasted sharply with my own overflow of sarcasm and despair.

So I went for it. In my pal Dave Musser's parents' living room, I asked Jesus into my life and vaulted forward into sheer euphoria. Gone was the burden of melancholy that had plagued me for months. Heaven itself had swept me up in its arms and for the next half-year seemed to carry me a foot off the ground.

What eventually brought me back to earth was the alarming question "What have I done?" That was followed closely by "Is Christianity even true?" I've spent the last thirty-five years working on that second question.

For many Christians, this is not a pressing matter. They feel secure in their faith, and if you ask them, "Why choose Christianity? Why not take a leap of faith into Islam or Buddhism or any other religion or worldview?" their response is, "I don't know. You just have to have faith in Christ."

For those who possess a simple faith born of their upbringing or their desperate need for Jesus or a kingdom community to belong to, I say more power to them. Some people seem to have the gift of faith, one that comes naturally. They don't need a lot of logic behind it. We could put a negative spin on their experience by calling it a blind leap into darkness, but I'd say it's mostly an instinctive move into divine light, an uncluttered response to the beckoning of God.

That's not how Emily saw things. For her there had to be solid reasons to back up her faith if it were ever to blossom. And I'm not like that either. I realized I needed to know the arguments, the rationale, the history, the evidence for something before placing my faith in it. Are there well-founded reasons for thinking Christianity is true?

If there were no valid reasons, or if the evidence turned against Christianity, I'd be gone. Outta here. I'd have to give up my job as a campus minister, stop going to church, stop praying, look elsewhere for meaning and just play more golf, I guess. I'm not the type to hang on to a falsehood just so I can milk it for emotional security. There's no true security in a fabrication.

Thus for many Christians like Emily and myself, faith comes in two stages: evidential and relational. The evidential stage is where we work through the rational case for Christ. It's mainly a cognitive process that consists of sifting through evidence and examining arguments, as if our minds were a court of law coming to a verdict about Christianity. If the verdict is positive, we're able to move forward with the relational stage, which involves making a personal commitment of love and trust in Jesus Christ.

Someone may object that the two stages of faith are not that neat and clean, and I agree. In the real world people move back and forth between the evidential and the relational sides of faith, similar to a budding romance that leads to marriage. When I was dating my wife Sharon, there was a period of two years when I was simultaneously falling in love while also mentally evaluating the evidence of her good character and loyalty (I admit, it sounds a little cold and calculating). It was all happening at the same time.

Nevertheless, even though the chronological order of the two faith stages is comingled, the logical order is not. Logically, solid evidence for Christ is a precondition for a relationship with Christ, at least for people like myself who are intellectually cautious and wish to avoid irrational commitments.

In the remainder of this chapter I will offer two concrete images that illustrate the evidential and relational stages of faith.

EVIDENTIAL STAGE IMAGE: SKYDIVING

Certain stories have incredible staying power in my mind, such as an account told to me many years ago by a woman whose husband died in a skydiving accident. I don't even remember her name (or his), but I've no problem recalling the details of the tragedy. It was in Florida. He leapt from a plane on a windy day, spiraled downward, pulled the ripcord, dangled under a full chute, appeared to be coming in for a soft two-point landing—but got entangled in power lines.

The image of skydiving illustrates the evidential stage of faith for several reasons. One is the risk of failure, as the above story illustrates.

How could faith possibly fail? Easy. If you place your faith in the wrong thing, it fails. After all, it's logically possible that Christianity is false and another worldview, such as Judaism or atheism, is true. And even though I may affirm the person whose faith comes naturally without much evidential support, it's only fair to acknowledge that such faith could in fact be misplaced.

I once asked a Mormon missionary how he knew his faith was true. He replied that when he was reading the Book of Mormon, God spoke to his heart, and he thus came to believe in the Mormon religion. This is sometimes called a "burning of the bosom," a sense that God is revealing himself through the Mormon scriptures. I pressed the matter further. How did he know it was actually God speaking to him and not some other spiritual being or even his own imagination? He just knew. But how? He'd simply opened his heart to the truth of the scriptures and now he was one hundred percent convinced. But—

You see the dilemma of a faith-only approach to truth, which is sometimes called "fideism" by scholars. Choosing the correct object of faith is the crucial thing. I've met people of all different religions (not to mention the irreligious) who hold their beliefs in a natural, organic, almost effortless way. It hardly occurs to them that their views could be false. Yet they cannot all be true. Religions such as

Christianity, Mormonism, Judaism and Buddhism make statements about reality that are in direct conflict with each other. For example, the Christian understanding of God as Trinity disagrees with the other religions just mentioned. Logically, someone (or everyone) is off base here.

But it's not just fideism that can fail. Those of us who work hard at the evidential part of faith have no guarantees that our cognitive pursuits will pay off. We can be tragically caught in the power lines of intellectualism. We can mishandle arguments, misinterpret data or cave in to our prejudices and wishful thinking. The supposed objective "court of law," which is our mind's judge and jury, may not function properly. When we jump out of the airplane of faith, faulty thinking can land us in the wrong spot.

Still, I'll take my chances with the evidence. To me there's nothing like thoroughly investigating a case for something before believing its claims. That's why I've spent the last three-plus decades asking the question of whether Christianity is true, digging through its historical, philosophical and experiential arguments. It's been a fantastic course of study! Again, I absolutely do not want to hold to a position that is false.

And hey, did you know that skydiving is relatively safe? It's easy to focus on the risk of failure, but what about the probabilities of success? Well, according to the U.S. Parachute Association, in 2010 only twenty-one fatalities occurred in its members' estimated three million jumps. That's a 99.993 percent safety record.

Before I'd ever jump out of an airplane, I'd read all the safety statistics and interview seasoned jumpers and check out every single piece of high-tech gear twice. That process is what I call the evidential part of skydiving. You look before you leap. You calculate the risks. And even though the evidence falls short of the high standard of proof, it's still pretty convincing.

Notice that so far in this argument about the first stage of faith, we've emphasized how evidence and rationale are important to many thoughtful Christians, but we haven't provided any evidence yet. That's okay. That will come later. An important lesson for apologists is to build the case for faith slowly, one brick at a time. The small but significant claim we're making here is that evidence matters to faith. That's it. No need to present the whole deal at once. Let the larger case for Christ unfold incrementally, establishing each minor point as a foundation for additional points to be made in the future.

A skeptic may have several responses to our modest presentation at this juncture. A common one is that evidence as I'm defining it via the skydiving image is not applicable to religion. I hear this objection all the time. But here is where we must be strong. Notice my strategy in the following conversation:

ME: My faith in Christ depends on solid evidence and rationale. It's like skydiving. There's lots of evidence, such as the quality of the jumping gear and the statistical record of the U.S. Parachute Association, to suggest that I'll live to tell about my experience, so I'm willing to risk my life for the thrill of it all. I admit there's no proof of my safety in this sport, just as there's no proof of the truth of Christianity. But the evidence and arguments for a leap of faith from an airplane are very convincing—enough, at least, to actually take the plunge.

SKEPTICAL FRIEND: That's fine, Rick, but you can't apply that same reasoning to religion. Religious faith, by definition, is purely subjective and is not supported by evidence. You're confusing faith and facts, religion and science. Religion is the realm of feelings, values and personal faith. Science is the realm of logic, evidence and reason. Don't get them mixed up.

ME: But *my* faith *is* supported by evidence. After all, it's *my* faith, *my* way of doing things. I would never place my faith in Christ unless there were plenty of evidence and arguments for doing so. I'm interested in an "informed" faith, not a blind faith. And you're not really in a position to tell me otherwise.

See what I just did? I've used a concrete image—skydiving—to make a memorable point that's essentially autobiographical—my faith, my story. I'm the one who skydives and who draws the parallel to faith in Christ, and I must not allow my skeptical friend to declare such a connection out of bounds.

If the first common response from skeptics is to attempt to disallow the analogy between faith and skydiving, the second is much more hopeful. The person simply says, "Okay then, show me the evidence."

This is exactly the response we're looking for because it means our friend has agreed to the idea that faith can, in principle, be supported by evidence. Never take this point for granted. Though it seems obvious to most Christians, atheists sometimes relegate the whole notion of faith into an airtight compartment that is cut off from rational processes.

But again, it's not their faith; it's ours. And we cannot allow them to define our faith for us. If our faith is "rational," that's our business. In public debates and in private conversations with atheists, I've said many times, "Don't impose your definition of faith on me. I'm not defending a version of Christianity that is based on blind faith. I'm defending faith that is shaped by reason, logic and evidence. I'm talking about informed faith, calculated risk."

For the skeptical friend who is in fact wanting to hear the evidence for the truth claims of Christianity, we're in great position to move the conversation forward in any number of directions. We can look at the historical evidence for the life of Jesus as presented in the four Gospels. We can talk about the philosophical, moral and scientific arguments that undergird the Christian faith. And most importantly, we can existentially demonstrate the love of Jesus to our friend and perhaps invite her to experience the supernatural manifestation of Christ himself, that being Christian community. These options are all fair game, and deciding on the right one(s) takes prayer and discernment.

Back to Emily. I remember my week at her campus. InterVarsity sponsored a talk on "The Problem of Suffering, Evil and a Good God." She was there. Same ambivalence in her manner. "Christianity and the Challenge of Other Religions" also brought her out, and in this talk she actually raised her hand and asked a question. That was progress. "Atheism and the Existence of God" was the talk where I saw a real change coming over Emily. She was fully engaged in the argument I'd drawn on the board and had no problem looking me directly in the eye.

Afterward, she approached me. "Can we talk?"

I grinned. "I was hoping you'd eventually say that."

She told me that Christianity was really making sense to her, that the reasons for believing in Jesus were falling into place. I asked if she had any lingering questions and she said no, not really. A few seconds of silence ensued as she stared past me. "Well then, are you ready?" I broke in.

"No."

As it turned out, Emily had other life issues holding her back from becoming a devoted Christ-follower, at least for the moment. Later, things changed. But at least she'd managed to clear the first significant barrier to faith—intellectual skepticism. The evidence and arguments had convinced her that Christianity was true. For now, however, she would remain inside the airplane, still contemplating the jump.

Our defining image for the first stage of Christian faith, then, is skydiving. Use this illustration in your spiritual conversations and it will help crystallize the idea that faith is not merely an arbitrary leap in the dark. We're talking about the difference between blind faith and informed faith. I'm all about informed faith. How about you?

THE RELATIONAL STAGE: A MARRIAGE

A few years ago I was meeting weekly for Bible study with a young woman at Hamline University in St. Paul. She had a fairly active church background but had never really closed the loop on her faith in Christ. So I asked her, "Sarah, I get the sense that you enjoy studying the Scriptures and want to follow God with your life. But I'm wondering, are you still merely dating Jesus, or have you taken that final step of getting married to him, spiritually speaking?"

Sarah knew what I meant. I was using the metaphor of a wedding to communicate the idea of a lifelong commitment of love to Jesus.

"Dating," she said simply, and smiled. I then challenged her to walk through a wedding service in her mind during the coming week and report back to me at our next appointment. She agreed.

Seven days later I slid into my usual booth in the student center where Sarah was waiting. After some chitchat I asked her gently if she'd taken any big spiritual steps since we'd last met.

"I did it," she said, with another smile.

"Tell me."

"I went out for a run and decided that I was ready, that the big day had finally arrived. So I stopped at a park bench and sat down, and in my mind I walked through this wedding ceremony, step by step. It began in the back of the church as I looked forward over the pews. Jesus was standing up front, waiting for me. So I made my way down the aisle and went to him. His hand was outstretched and I took it. We stated our vows together. I said, 'I do,' and now, well, I guess I'm married."

Okay, I was toast. Through moist eyes I mumbled some sort of "congratulations" and just sat there, stunned by this magnificent moment.

"There's more," she said. Yikes. I couldn't take anymore. "Another runner saw me on the park bench crying and asked if I was okay or needed any help. 'No. This is the happiest day of my life!' I told him. He looked a little confused, then ran off."

This was rapidly becoming one of my happiest days as well.

The image of marriage for conversion to Christ works at several levels, and I'd recommend the image to you. The first is the obvious step of making a defined, formal step of faith. Before the ceremony Sarah was "not married" to Jesus, and then after her I-do's she became "officially" married. It's not that she didn't have a notion of faith or love before the ceremony, but at the altar she really sealed the deal.

For evangelism and apologetics this is an important final step. We need to clarify the idea of conversion for our non-Christian friends so they know exactly what's expected of them, and the idea of matrimony is perfect: it's easy to remember, it's common rather than obscure, it's concrete rather than abstract, it's an event that generally evokes warm feelings (though not always), and most of all it's easy for us to communicate—quickly, if need be.

Plus, it fits with Scripture's overall teaching about God being united to his people in covenant marriage. A sampling includes Isaiah 62:5, where God, the bridegroom, rejoices over Israel, his bride; Mark 2:18-20, where Jesus depicts himself as the bridegroom of his followers; and 2 Corinthians 11:2, where Paul states that he has promised to give the church to one husband: Christ.

In the end, we must of course share the whole gospel with non-Christians, which includes elements such as repentance and counting the cost. Inside that larger message, however, there's nothing like a tangible, memorable image to capture and summarize larger truths, thus planting a seed in the minds of our hearers that, God willing, will grow and flourish into full-blown faith. Jesus often used concrete images such as seed, birds, bread, water and money to connect with his audience. These metaphors are embedded in Gospel stories that many of us can recite on cue. Abstract propositions, by contrast, are a lot tougher to present and definitely tougher to comprehend (and subsequently recall) for listeners.

The marriage image works on other levels as well. Back to the first stage of faith, which is evidential: I often state in evangelistic conversations and public talks that I have every reason to believe that my wife, Sharon, loves me and is faithful to our marriage. But there's no proof. I can't put love under a microscope. In fact, isn't it the case that many times a husband or wife is the last one to know about an illicit relationship carried on by his or her spouse?

It seems to me that atheists and other skeptics who demand proof of things before they're willing to act do, in fact, trust and love their spouses and friends without having anything like proof. Evidence, yes. Philosophical-scientific certitude, no. It's the same with my faith in Jesus. There's tons of evidence that compels me to go to the altar and pledge my devotion and loyalty to him.

In summary, those are the two stages of faith, at least for myself and many other Christians. The evidential stage is crystallized in the skydiving metaphor, the relational stage in the marriage metaphor. Use these two images and you'll be on your way to apologetic conversations that are crisp, focused and, with God's help, convincing.

By the way, I found out a few months after my visit to Emily's campus that she'd disentangled herself from a downer boyfriend and devoted her life to Jesus Christ.

PLAY YOUR WHOLE ORCHESTRA

The Cumulative Case for Faith

THE YEAR I BECAME A CHRISTIAN, 1976, is the year author James Sire wrote *The Universe Next Door: A Basic Worldview Catalog*.[1] I was nineteen. The book revolutionized my thinking. It gave me a framework for understanding the differences in how people think about the great questions of life, such as origins, meaning and purpose, the existence of God and what happens after death.

At age twenty-four I joined the staff of InterVarsity Christian Fellowship, and a few years later found myself living in the Minneapolis area with my family and inviting Dr. Sire to speak at the University of Minnesota and nearby Macalester College. He had taken his book and his vast knowledge of literature and philosophy on the road to serve InterVarsity as a traveling apologist. I remember sitting in a Macalester dorm lounge one evening with Dr. Sire and a group of students. He'd been doing his case making, which was appropriately on the intellectual side of things, when a student asked whether Christian faith didn't involve more than logic and rationality. I'll never forget Sire's answer: "Yes, much more!" he said enthusiastically. Then he paused and added, "But never *less*."

I resolved at the time to never shrink from being thoughtful about faith, certainly not to settle for what is often called in the church "heart knowledge." But of course faith is never less than that, either. It's both: head and heart, reason and affection. No doubt C. S. Lewis's continued popularity is due largely to his ability to touch the humanity of his readers at multiple levels, from mind (*Mere Christianity*) to imagination (*The Chronicles of Narnia*) to heart (*A Grief Observed*). Lewis's whole approach suggests a well-rounded spirituality that I desire for myself—and you.

Fast-forward about twenty years to 2009. I made a dinner appointment in Madison, Wisconsin, with Dr. Sire in order to seek his counsel for my next career move inside InterVarsity. He'd been gradually retiring from his worldwide tour of duties as an apologist, and I was just starting out in that field. In the course of our conversation he asked if I'd ever thought of using my musical abilities in my apologetics work. The question surprised me. I'd never considered such a thing. The veteran apologist was thinking outside the box—at least my box—and I must confess, the idea of a musical apologetic seemed a bit dainty for the rugged warfare I imagined lay ahead.

But for Sire, everything in the universe is a potential apologetic for the truth of Jesus Christ, music being no exception. He holds to the radical notion that philosophy, literature, science, medicine, art, recreation, beauty, relationships—shall I go on?—everything in its own way points to God. You can put me down for that as well. I'm in on the "everything" part of the universe aiming Godward. It's like saying that every element in a painting refers in some sense to its painter.

THE CUMULATIVE CASE

Based on this expanded understanding of apologetics, I want to suggest to you the value of using a cumulative-case approach in your conversations with seekers and skeptics. This case is made up of many little steps that build on each other and interlock to form a coherent (and persuasive) whole. It's based on the underlying idea that all truth is God's truth, wherever it may be found. Thus you are free to use philosophy, art, personal experience—whatever—to make your appeal to a friend who doesn't know Christ.

And if you believe as I do that all God's truth fits together with itself like a puzzle, then no matter what little piece of it you share with another person, that piece will necessarily interlock with all the other pieces. And every piece you subsequently add to the conversation will strengthen your overall case. This is the approach that philosopher Douglas Groothuis takes in his massive *Christian Apologetics: A Comprehensive Case for Biblical Faith*, in which he makes his arguments for Christianity from a variety of philosophical, historical and experiential angles—all of which "combine several types of arguments to form a cumulative-case . . . that is stronger than the force of any argument taken by itself."[2]

For example, Christians routinely bring together two disparate worlds in their everyday life: history and psychology. How? They believe there was a real historical figure, Jesus Christ, the Son of God, who died on a cross and rose victorious over death. The psychology part comes in when Christians receive forgiveness for their sins from this Jesus. Forgiveness is great for the psyche! But in Christianity, forgiveness depends on the reality of a historical Jesus and true moral guilt. Thus a piece of history and a piece of psychology fit together. When a person outside the faith begins to see this comprehensive picture of God's world and all its interlocking pieces, it can be revolutionary.

Another way to think about the cumulative case is to consider how a prosecuting attorney goes about her business. She marshals together converging lines of evidence to convince a jury that the defendant is guilty. These lines of evidence may involve witnesses, circumstances, a weapon, phone records, a motive and the like. Taken alone, any of these elements is important but probably will not carry the day. Rather, it's the cumulative effect of the ideas and data—what theologian James Beilby describes as "piecing together a series of converging arguments and evidences"[3]—that is likely to bring a conviction. If I'm a juror, show me a weapon and I just shrug. But show me a weapon tied to a motive and you've captured my attention.

THE DEFINING IMAGE: A SYMPHONY ORCHESTRA

In conversation with skeptics, a helpful image you can use for the cumulative case is a symphony orchestra. This analogy quickly shows the breadth of the argument you are attempting to make for Christian faith. It suggests that you probably don't have a single silver-bullet argument that, properly understood, would convince any reasonable person of the truth of Jesus Christ. More likely, you'll be presenting Christianity one section at a time.[4] The word "section" here is meant as a continuation of the orchestra metaphor, referring to strings, wind instruments, brass and percussion. Of course you can always change the orchestra analogy to marching band, rock band, jazz combo—whatever you know best.

So let's say a friend asks for evidence for the supposed truth of the New Testament. You respond by letting the brass section play up the historical evidence for the reliability of ancient New Testament texts (see chapters five and six). This evidence may include a "trumpet" performing something about first-century Christian sources and a "French horn" adding important information about early non-Christian sources. You can proceed in this piecemeal fashion on any major issue, such as religious pluralism, the problem of suffering and evil, or origins. Different sections or subsections of the orchestra perform different parts of your case on each of these (and many other) topics.

In the deep background of these symphonic resources is the notion that God himself remains active in the wide world, across all disciplines and traditions. Author Andy Crouch asks, "Is the Maker of the world still at work 'changing the world'? . . . What would it mean to join him in what he is doing in every sphere and scale of human culture?"[5] An implication here is that we don't actually bring God into any section of the orchestra but that he is already there, speaking (playing) his truth from every angle imaginable. Our job as his partners is simply to showcase his music in all its astonishing variety.

At this point you may be wondering what the big deal is—why we even need an analogy for this idea of coming at issues from different angles. It seems too obvious and not in any way remarkable or profound.

Hold on. It gets more interesting. Here's where you really need to dig into the analogy: Many skeptics disallow certain sections of the orchestra to perform at all, defining them out of the conversation before a single note is played. They will tell you that unless your statements are confined to a specific narrow range of argumentation, you're not really making a legitimate argument for anything.

For example, a pretty common restriction I hear on college campuses is that unless I provide objective, unbiased, scientific evidence for Christianity, I'm literally talking about nothing at all. So let's say I break out the violins and play up my personal experience with the risen Christ. The skeptic will object that I'm being too subjective. Subjective arguments are out of play, he insists, because lots of people have subjective, mystical experiences with a variety of religions and spiritualities, and there's no way to judge between them all.

Okay, you see what just happened? Boundaries have been set, and if I cave in to the boundaries stipulated by a skeptic, I'll probably go down in flames. Inside his playing field I have very little chance of making my case. But if the playing field is a lot wider than what my skeptical friend says, maybe we can get somewhere.

So part of my witness is the decision to hold my ground on the question of width. The symphony orchestra analogy will help you remember in the middle of a conversation that you are well within your rights to let all the instruments perform. And if at some point a skeptical friend simply will not engage with anything except, say, the flutes, you have two choices: play those flutes to the max and be content, or call a stalemate. The latter option is necessary at times, in which case you have little to do but pray that the Lord may still bring him around to hear the rest of your symphony at some point.

USING THE CUMULATIVE CASE

A few years ago I was invited to take part in a friendly give-and-take—something between a panel discussion and a debate—on the topic of the historical Jesus. My pal Lee gave his skeptical perspective on Jesus, and I gave my believing perspective, then we went back and forth a bit, live. I guess it was a debate after all. Then we fielded questions from the audience of about fifty folks, mostly leaning toward Lee's side and mostly directed toward me.

Amazingly, almost none of the questions pertained to the historical Jesus. I remember getting questions on the Trinity, ethics, hypocrisy, evolution, faith versus science, Bible contradictions, the wrath of God—and yes, it was fun! And yes, I was a little shaky at first. But I found my chops early on and played every instrument in my orchestra, including that of interpersonal connection (my "saxophone") at a bar afterward with about twenty skeptics.

One guy at the bar went after me hard about the Bible being self-contradictory because it prohibits incest and yet incestuous relations were the only method available for Cain to bear children (Genesis 4:17). What do you say to that? As it turned out he didn't really want to know my opinion but rather wanted to release his pent-up objections to a captive Christian audience—me in this case.[6] The guy's pushy manner caused a couple of other skeptics to intervene and offer apologies to me, which warmed the conversation considerably and established personal connections with them.

I remember thinking to myself on the drive home that I'd spoken of philosophy, theology, history and science that evening. I'd referred to art, literature and the ministry of my church, and, of course, I'd shared my personal testimony of knowing and loving Jesus. When I'd gotten to the more subjective, even sentimental parts (violins) of my case, a few skeptical eyes in the audience had glazed over. Too bad for them; they missed out on gold.

Fact is, I am a human being created in the image of God. That means I ought to have as wide-ranging an interest in knowledge and culture as God does. That may be a slight hyperbole, but I'm simply suggesting that as little replicas or "mirrors" of the God of all truth, we ought to be about the business of learning God's truth wherever it resides and communicating it to a hurting, dying world. That means I need to bring my entire self, complete with full-piece orchestra, to every evangelistic encounter I'm given. And I'm not going to let a skeptic tell me that certain sections of my orchestra are not allowed on the premises. After all, skeptics are also made in the image of God—heart, soul, mind and body—and who can tell what instrument God might use to reach them with his truth and love?[7]

POSTSCRIPT

During a talk I gave at Michigan State University, I happened to mention that I'd grown up playing music, and I just happened to flash on the screen a couple of boyhood photos of my brothers and me as teenage entertainers in the seventies—decked out in chartreuse costumes, of course! After the talk there was a short Q&A time, and one of the young Spartans asked a question I can honestly say I'd never been asked before: "Would you sing us a song?"

I thought about it for two seconds, glanced over at the worship leader who gave me the nod, and picked up her acoustic guitar. Sing? No. But I played the hymn, "When I Survey the Wondrous Cross," without screwing up the tricky fingerings even once. Something different about Jesus was communicated in those three minutes, different from anything I'd said the prior half-hour. I'd forgotten that a guitar could be part of my symphony orchestra. What are your instruments?

SUGGESTED RESOURCES

Alex McLellan, *A Jigsaw Guide to Making Sense of the World* (Downers Grove, IL: InterVarsity Press, 2012).

Douglas Groothuis, *Christian Apologetics: A Comprehensive Case for Biblical Faith* (Downers Grove, IL: InterVarsity Press, 2011).

Andy Crouch, *Culture Making: Recovering Our Creative Calling* (Downers Grove, IL: InterVarsity Press, 2008).

3

HOW THE WORLD CAME TO BE

The Grand Designer

I BELIEVE IN GOD, because the universe had to come from somewhere."

I was sitting in the stands of a youth basketball game with Chad, a fellow parent. You can only gush over your kids and complain about the referees so much before matters of greater concern arise.

"God in general, or a specific god?" I asked.

"Don't know. All religions are pretty much the same. I just figure God—whoever he or she is—got the world started. After that, who knows?"

Chad didn't believe in any specific religion. For him, the point was that there was a creator. There had to be. The world couldn't cause itself; it couldn't just pop into existence. Of that much Chad was sure.

In my travels to college campuses around the country, it's not unusual to hear students express sentiments similar to Chad's. They may not be affiliated with any particular church or religion, but they believe in God as a matter of course. Certainly atheist and agnostic students are increasing in number. Nevertheless, for the vast majority, belief in a deity provides an intuitive, common-sense explanation for how the cosmos came into being, something that Christians affirm as being true.[1]

Cosmology, which is the study of the origin of the world, is the focus of this chapter. Specifically, I'll try to show why God is the best explanation for the existence of the universe, and I'll offer one central image—God as a grand designer—as well as three minor images you can put to use in conversation.

To begin, in my travels I encounter three main worldviews in the university. A worldview is a lens through which a person interprets the world. The three views are theism, pantheism and naturalism: the God lens, the god lens and the no-god lens. These categories are perhaps oversimplified, but I find them helpful—not because they encompass all the views out there (they don't), but because they're easy to remember and they're actually representative of ninety percent of the students and faculty I meet on college campuses.

Figure 1.

Notice that in theism God stands outside the universe, while in pantheism god *is* the universe, and of course in naturalism the universe is all there is. Representative examples of each worldview are Christianity, Hinduism and atheism. I'll confine myself to talking about Christianity and atheism in this chapter. Other theists such as Jews and Muslims will find large areas of overlap with their own beliefs in the discussion.

THE GRAND DESIGNER

For Christians, God can be seen as a kind of grand designer who conceived of the structure and beauty of the universe and created it out of nothing. This creative act is what theologians refer to as *ex nihilo*—"out of nothing," meaning that God didn't use any preexisting materials, nor did he create the universe out of his own being. Rather, the universe "wasn't" there, then it "was." God spoke it into existence.

British philosopher Richard Swinburne believes that God provides a complete explanation for the phenomena we observe in the world. The complexity, beauty and vastness of the universe, the animated life forms of plants and animals, and the pinnacle of creation—human beings, understood as moral, relational, intelligent beings—all point to a creator, a grand designer whose nature is stamped indelibly into the fabric of the cosmos. Swinburne thinks this is just what we'd expect to find if something like the God of Christianity existed.[2] When we look around, we see not only the world itself but something of the world-maker.

This reminds me of my elderly friend Marion, whose husband passed away a few years ago. She once said to me that she sees Johnnie in the house all the time—not his physical or apparitional presence, but his jacket, his favorite chair, his arrangement of things. His signature, written lovingly into these items, is still visible to the person who knows what to look for.

THREE OPTIONS

Not everyone thinks God is a good explanation for things. I remember meeting Kevin during an outreach event at a state school in the Midwest. Our ministry had set up camp in a high-traffic area of the student union, and we were asking passersby what they thought of religion. "Done with it" was Kevin's response. I found out that he'd grown up in the church but, like many of his peers, had divorced himself from the faith while in college. He'd been studying other religions and their worship spaces (temples, mosques) and had come to believe that the parity between religions had a canceling effect on all of them. If all religions claimed to be true, most likely none of them were.

Where did the universe come from? "Not sure," Kevin said. "Not from God. Probably always there, or else the Big Bang."

That's a great summary from Kevin. Here are the choices:

1. The universe had a beginning and was caused by God or some other force. Or:

2. The universe always existed. Matter is eternal. Or:

3. The universe had a beginning and was self-caused—probably the Big Bang.

We could mention other alternatives as well, but these are the main ones. Christianity embraces the first option. What's wrong with the other two?

The second statement, that the universe always existed, runs into a few problems. One is that we don't normally think of objects in the world as being able to create themselves or otherwise cause themselves to exist. Things are brought into existence by prior conditions and forces. A tree is "caused" by seeds derived from prior trees, which are themselves the product of prior trees, and so forth. This chain of existence is true for everything and everyone in the universe. It all goes back in time along a sequence of cause-effect relationships, back to the beginning, to the very first cause of things.

But in an eternal universe there is no "first cause." Rather, things regress forever. Philosophers refer to this as an "infinite regress," and many think it's an irrational concept. What critique can we make of the infinite regress? Kreeft and Tacelli provide an analogy about trying to borrow a book that doesn't exist:

Existence is like a gift given from cause to effect. If there is no one who has the gift, the gift cannot be passed down the chain of receivers, however long or short the chain may be. If everyone has to borrow a certain book, but no one actually *has* it, then no one will ever *get* it. If there is no God who has existence by his own eternal nature, then the gift of existence cannot be passed down the chain of creatures and we can never get it. But we do get it; we exist. Therefore there must exist a God: an Uncaused Being who does not have to receive existence like us—and like every other link in the chain of receivers.[3]

I like that image. You can never borrow a book if no one has the book. You can never receive the gift of existence if no one has that gift to give. You can never have a whole series of cause-effect relationships if the series has no starting point. It is fair to ask what (or who) caused the whole series.

The third option, that the universe had a beginning and was self-caused or caused by the Big Bang, also runs into difficulties. The most obvious is how something could come from nothing. If there is absolutely nothing there—where "nothing" is defined not as some kind of substance in itself but as a lack of anything—how could a lack of anything bring about something?[4] Something like a universe?

In *The Case for a Creator*, Lee Strobel recounts his own reckoning with this question:

> Looking at the doctrine of Darwinism, which undergirded my atheism for so many years, it didn't take me long to conclude that it was simply too far-fetched to be credible. I realized that if I were to embrace Darwinism and its underlying premise of naturalism, I would have to believe that:
>
> • Nothing produces everything
> • Non-life produces life . . .
> • Unconsciousness produces consciousness
> • Non-reason produces reason
>
> Based on this, I was forced to conclude that Darwinism would require a blind leap of faith that I was not willing to make.[5]

Scientific explanations assume something already exists—some form of matter and energy. But we're trying to get beyond those first forms to the "nothing" part of this discussion. The nothing-to-something transition seems a topic best suited for philosophy or theology rather than science. It's that mystery I'm asking the skeptic to explain.

To illustrate, I hold a rock in my hand and show it to students. I ask if the rock can cause itself to exist. Obviously not. But what if we made the rock bigger—into a planet, for example? It still cannot cause its own existence. The analogy proceeds to bigger objects—a solar system, a galaxy, finally the universe. Can a universe cause itself to exist? Spring into being from nothing? One would think not.

SKEPTICAL OBJECTIONS

Atheists and other skeptics have plenty of objections to these arguments. Perhaps the most common is to argue that it's quite rational to believe in an eternal universe: "Why not?" the skeptic thinks. The world was always there, or God was always there—what's the difference? Same idea. Besides, God is really no ultimate solution. If God made the world, who made God?[6]

I am sympathetic to this objection because Christians often press skeptics for ultimate and final explanations of things. Then when the skeptic cannot produce such a solution, the Christian says, "Aha! If only you had God, this problem would be solved." So it is natural for the skeptic to return the favor and ask for an ultimate explanation of theism that includes God.

But as William Lane Craig argues, "In order to recognize an explanation as the best, one needn't have an explanation of the explanation."[7] So let's say a coworker who's been sick comes back to work and finds a new printer in the office. She asks me where it came from and I tell her we purchased it from the local office-supply store. In order to accept my explanation, she obviously doesn't need to know where the office-supply store came from. This is a simple matter of sticking to the issue at hand. I tell skeptics in this situation, "I gave you an explanation for the universe. I thought that's what we were talking about. If you also want an explanation for God, that's a different question."[8]

As for the mysteries of the Big Bang being solved by science, I doubt it. Science will give us much insight[9]—and we as Christians should support such efforts—but the metaphysical move from "nothing" to "something" is a question for philosophy and theology. And that's where God comes in. As Swinburne points out, "The most general phenomenon that provides evidence for the existence of God is the existence of the physical universe. . . . This is something evidently inexplicable by science. . . . What science by its very nature cannot explain is why there are any states of affairs at all."[10]

CONVERSATIONS WITH SKEPTICS

When it comes to apologetic dialogue, it's okay to make a good case for something and have it rejected by non-Christians. Our job as evangelists-apologists is not to present irrefutable arguments. Few, if any, exist anyway. Rather, our job is to present an attractive, alternative universe to seekers and skeptics. What I'm inviting a non-Christian friend to consider is a different way of looking at life, a way that has been embraced by billions of people for two thousand years, a way that has changed countless lives, including my own.

So even though I think the arguments for the existence of God are sound and convincing, the other person may not. And at that point I must simply let go. I need to say my piece and trust the Holy Spirit to work. Yes, I want to make the God case as persuasively as possible. I put all-out effort into the conversation. But in the end I have to remember that I'm not responsible for other people. They are responsible for their own standing before God, and God is responsible for granting "eyes to see" and "ears to hear." My only responsibility is to be the messenger—in a caring and prayerful way. The rest is out of my hands.

A DOUBTER

Paul and I were shooting hoops at the gym when a discussion about the Big Bang emerged out of nowhere. One minute we were joking about my lack of skill in dribbling, passing and rebounding, then boom: "Where did the world come from?" It was a head-spinning non sequitur.

Paul is a chin-rubbing doubter. He says, "Mmmm" a lot. Once we were into the topic of cosmology, I mentioned that I didn't think the world could have come into existence from nothing but needed something outside itself to get it going: God. Paul pondered that idea, looking dubious. "Rick, you say God was always there. I say the world was always there. What's the difference?"

"The world is a thing. Things can't cause their own existence. Look at this basketball. Could it make itself?"

"A crude example," Paul said, scratching his goatee. "The ball was made by people. That says nothing about the world."

"Ah, but it does. The ball needed something outside itself, some non-thing or personal agency to manufacture it. That's my analogy for the earth, which is a big ball, or the universe, which is the biggest object imaginable. These things needed some sort of designer to think them up and bring them into existence."

"You haven't told me where this supposed designer came from, Rick. If it's God, who made God?"

"Paul, are you saying that you won't believe Wilson Sporting Goods manufactured this basketball unless I tell you where Wilson came from? And if I have to account for Wilson, then what about the backgrounds of all the employees at Wilson—and their parents, grandparents, great-grandparents and so forth? No explanation at any point in the series would be sufficient, because you could always say, 'Okay, but where did they come from?' I thought the main idea here was just to give an account of the ball."

"Mmmm. I'll have to think about that one."

I wish I could say that Paul saw the light in all this and fell to his knees in repentance before the Creator, but that's not the case. Nevertheless, I hope you get the gist of the analogy about the rock—which in this case was a basketball. It doesn't count as a full-blown argument against a purely natural, secular understanding of cosmology, but it helps make your point about a creator of the world more concrete and memorable. The rest of the "convincing" in a friend's mind and heart is up to the Lord.

CHAPTER SUMMARY

The overarching image	The grand designer: God designed and created the universe out of nothing. And following Richard Swinburne, we look around the world and say to ourselves, "This is exactly the type of world one would expect to find if there is a God."
When skeptics say this:	**Reply like this:**
The world is eternal.	The book analogy: An eternal world is like an infinite regress. Every effect has a prior cause, but unfortunately there is no first cause to get it all going. It's like a book that everyone needs to borrow, but if no one ever had the book in the first place, it can never be lent or borrowed.
The world is self-caused through the Big Bang.	The rock image: Hold a real or imaginary rock in your hand and ask whether the rock can cause itself to exist. Then move to larger versions of the rock — the planet, solar system, galaxy and universe. None of these can cause their own existence. It takes God to do that.
Who made God?	The new copier: A colleague returns to work after an absence and finds a new copier in the office. She asks where it came from and I tell her from the office-supply store. She can accept my explanation without asking where the office-supply store came from. In the same way, we're offering an explanation for the existence of the universe, not God. God, by definition, is self-existent, which is a related but separate issue.

SUGGESTED RESOURCES

William Lane Craig, "Dawkins's Delusion," in *Contending with Christianity's Critics: Answering New Atheists and Other Objectors*, ed. Paul Copan and William Lane Craig (Nashville: B&H Academic, 2009).

C. Stephen Evans and R. Zachary Manis, *Philosophy of Religion: Thinking About Faith*, 2nd ed. (Downers Grove, IL: IVP Academic, 2009), pp. 66-67.

Douglas Groothuis, *Christian Apologetics: A Comprehensive Case for Biblical Faith* (Downers Grove, IL: IVP Academic, 2011), chap. 11.

Lee Strobel, *The Case for a Creator: A Journalist Investigates Scientific Evidence That Points Toward God* (Grand Rapids, MI: Zondervan, 2005).

Ravi Zacharias and Norman Geisler, *Who Made God? And Answers to Over 100 Other Tough Questions of Faith* (Grand Rapids, MI: Zondervan, 2003), chap. 1.

4

THE WORLD IS LIKE A ROYAL FLUSH

A Case for the Design of the Universe

ONE OF THE THINKERS who's long intrigued me is the late British philosopher and famous atheist Antony Flew. When I first read his essay "The Presumption of Atheism," it opened up a world of dialogue for me with atheists and other skeptics by helping me understand their starting points. Flew's writings in general sound fair-minded to my ear. He was known for his dogged commitment to following the evidence wherever it led, regardless of the consequences to his reputation. Flew sought the truth. Period. And I could see from his interactions with the world's top philosophers of religion and science that he was one of the most respected thinkers of the twentieth century. He certainly had my respect.

At the moment I'm holding in my hands a collection of Flew's essays published under the 1993 title *Atheistic Humanism*. His short section on whether God designed the world includes this statement: "[The] Argument to Design, like all its predecessors, is . . . much too weak to prove the existence of such an infinite, omniscient, and omnipotent God." And in the "Presumption of Atheism" essay mentioned above, Flew objects to what he thinks is the disconnect between a "flawless Creator" and a creation flawed by sin.

In short, Flew is arguing that the hypothesis of God as "intelligent designer" of the world is mistaken. Surely a perfect God, if he exists, would have created a more perfect world.

Imagine my surprise when I learned that Flew had changed his mind. Around 2004, he'd come to believe in God. Not the God of the Bible, but something more in line with the God of Aristotle—a prime mover or "first cause" of the universe. This God did not call out a people for his own or send his Son to die for sins, and he does not answer prayer. But he did design the universe in all its astonishing ordered complexity and left us to discover its secrets. Flew came to his new belief by what he calls a "pilgrimage of reason and not of faith."[1]

In 2008 an aging Flew wrote a book with Roy Abraham Varghese titled *There Is a God: How the World's Most Notorious Atheist Changed His Mind.* Critics questioned whether the work was authentically Flew, but the great philosopher was careful to affirm his authorship of the book after its publication.

On the question of intelligent design, the Flew of 2004 and beyond was quite different from his former atheistic self: "I now believe that the universe was brought into existence by an infinite Intelligence. I believe that this universe's intricate laws manifest what scientists have called the Mind of God. I believe that life and reproduction originate in a divine Source."[2]

What is the argument from design, and why did Flew finally find it so convincing?[3] In the remainder of the chapter I will give two versions of the argument, along with two analogies for conversation. Then I'll mention several objections to intelligent design and offer brief replies to each.

DESIGN ARGUMENT 1: FINE-TUNING

As science has advanced in recent decades, a certain design argument called "fine-tuning" has become prominent.[4] It says that in order for the universe as we know it to be inhabitable by human beings and other life, "the laws of nature, the fundamental parameters of physics, and the initial conditions of the universe" must fall within certain narrow ranges.[5] And it's the combination of these many finely tuned properties that advocates of design point to as being fantastically improbable without God.

What are these finely tuned properties? Physicist and philosopher Robin Collins summarizes five:

1. If the initial explosion of the Big Bang had differed in strength by as little as one part in 1,060, the universe would have either quickly collapsed back on itself or expanded too rapidly for stars to form.

2. If the strong nuclear force, the force that binds protons and neutrons together in an atom, had been stronger or weaker by as little as five percent, life would be impossible.

3. If gravity had been stronger or weaker by one part in 1,040, then life-sustaining stars like the sun could not exist. This would most likely make life impossible.

4. If the neutron were not about 1.001 times the mass of the proton, all protons would have decayed into neutrons or all neutrons would have decayed into protons, and thus life would not be possible.

5. If the electromagnetic force were slightly stronger or weaker, life would be impossible.[6] John Jefferson Davis adds that if the force were stronger, "no planets would have formed and all stars would have been red dwarfs."[7]

Expanding this list, astronomer Hugh Ross in *Mere Creation* offers fifty-five parameters that are necessary to permit advanced life somewhere in the universe.[8] Twelve of the parameters pertaining to Earth are summarized below. It should be noted that not all scientists agree with Ross's list, and certainly many do not think there's an intelligent designer behind it all; nevertheless, few disagree that the universe does in fact exhibit extensive fine-tuning, whatever the cause. The following dozen items by themselves are impressive, in my opinion, and memorizing a few could prove useful in conversation with skeptics.

The number in parentheses after each item is the probability of that parameter falling in the required life-permitting range.

1. *Axis tilt (0.3)*. If greater, surface temperature differences on the planet would be too extreme for life to exist.

2. *Surface gravity (0.001) (escape velocity)*. If stronger, the planet's atmosphere would retain too much ammonia and methane. If weaker, the planet's atmosphere would lose too much water.

3. *Jupiter mass and distance from Earth (0.01)*. If the distance were greater or the mass less, too many asteroid and comet collisions would occur on Earth. If the mass were greater or the distance less, the Earth's orbit would become unstable.

4. *Water vapor level in the atmosphere (0.01)*. If greater, a runaway greenhouse effect would develop. If less, rainfall would be too meager for advanced life on the land.

5. *Quantity of forest and grass fires (0.1)*. If too many, there would be too much destruction of plant and animal life. If too few, not enough charcoal would be returned to soil, limiting biomass and diversity of life.

6. *Ozone level in atmosphere (0.01)*. If greater, surface temperatures would be too low. If less, surface temperatures would be too high; there would be too much ultraviolet radiation at the surface.

7. *Volcanic activity (0.1)*. If greater, too many life forms would be destroyed. If less, not enough carbon dioxide and water would be released into the atmosphere.

8. *Global distribution of continents (0.3)*. If too much in the southern hemisphere, seasonal differences would be too severe for advanced life.

9. *Thickness of crust (0.01).* If thicker, too much oxygen would be transferred from the atmosphere to the crust. If thinner, volcanic and tectonic activity would be too great.

10. *Oceans-to-continents ratio (0.2):* If greater, diversity and complexity of life forms would be limited. If smaller, diversity and complexity of life forms would be limited.

11. *Carbon dioxide level in atmosphere (0.01).* If greater, a runaway greenhouse effect would develop. If less, plants would be unable to maintain efficient photosynthesis.

12. *Oxygen quantity in atmosphere (0.01).* If greater, plants and hydrocarbons would burn up too easily. If less, advanced animals would have too little to breathe.

As much as any single parameter is unlikely, the real power of the evidence for fine-tuning is in their cumulative effect—of all occurring simultaneously. In *Mere Creation,* Ross estimates the probability of all fifty-five parameters being actualized as 10^{-69} and that a single planet in the universe meeting all the requirements has one chance in one hundred billion trillion.

Now let's say we're naturally cautious with such claims, so we factor in skeptics' differing interpretations of the relevant data, and we recognize that scientific theories are susceptible to modification as new discoveries are made. Let's say we go overboard with such caution and reduce the odds to half of what Ross is claiming, or we just delete one of the "trillions" in his estimate. Even on a pared-down claim—and I'm only suggesting this for rhetorical reasons when talking with skeptics—the fine-tuning of the universe and planet Earth is mind-blowing.

Collins thinks of fine-tuning as a series of radio dials, all of which must be set exactly right for life to be possible.[9] In his essay "The Teleological Argument: an Exploration of the Fine-Tuning of the Universe," he develops in detail six examples of fine-tuning,[10] each of which is independent of the others and each falling coincidentally (if by chance) within very narrow ranges. Alvin Plantinga estimates the odds of all six "radio dials" being tuned to life-permitting conditions as 10^{-100}.[11]

In trying to comprehend such a figure, Collins suggests thinking of the galaxy as a giant dartboard. By pure chance, a randomly thrown dart must hit a single one-foot square on the board—otherwise, life is impossible. "The fact that the dials are perfectly set, or that the dart has hit the target, strongly suggests that someone set the dials or aimed the dart, for it seems enormously improbable that such a coincidence could have happened by chance."[12]

Flew and Varghese observe that "the laws of nature seem to have been crafted so as to move the universe toward the emergence and sustenance of life."[13] Translation: Someone prepared a house for humanity to inhabit.

The royal flush analogy. Most skeptics who reject fine-tuning arguments are likely wary of coincidences in other areas of life, things that are too good to be true. "Randomly selected" by a marketing firm to win a prize every time you click on their website? Not likely. The same man shows up in five different airports on five different trips and sits close to you reading a newspaper? Not coincidental. As a fan of espionage and crime novels, for example, I can tell you that any international spy or local detective worth her salt looks on coincidences as clues to some design or intention. Spooks and cops trade on suspicion and distrust, the very tendencies of skepticism to which the royal flush analogy is aimed.[14]

So let's say someone shuffles a deck of cards and deals you a royal flush (for those of you less familiar with cards, a royal flush is the ace, king, queen, jack and ten of the same suit—the hand of the highest possible value in poker).[15] The odds of getting such a hand are one in 649,740, but so what? Once in a blue moon it happens. The deck is shuffled a second time, the cards are dealt and . . . whoa, two in a row. Then it happens again. And again. And again—that makes five consecutive royal flushes. It happens a hundred times in a row. The odds are nearly incalculable. Heck, after only the third flush you were starting to get suspicious. A Cubs World Series victory is surely more probable.

Someone is manipulating the cards.

This string of consecutive big flushes screams with each successive occurrence that "random chance" is not the best explanation here. In the same way, the complexity and fine-tuning of the universe is just too good to be true. Someone—not something—has a hand in shaping all this order. We call this someone God.

DESIGN ARGUMENT 2: CLASSIC INTELLIGENT DESIGN

The design argument from fine-tuning seems to be enjoying the most popularity in recent years. But a more general form of the case for intelligent design, which has a longer history, can also be mentioned.[16] In summary: When we look at the world around us, whether nature or human beings, there seems to be a lot of beneficial order. The laws of physics, the orderly motions of the stars and planets, the staggering complexity and efficiency of the human body and its many synchronized systems—these appear to be the work of a designer.

Evans and Manis put the argument succinctly:

1. There exist in nature many examples of beneficial order.

2. Beneficial order is best explained as the result of an intelligent designer.

3. Therefore, nature is probably the result of an intelligent designer.[17]

The watch analogy. As an image for the classic argument from design, I'd suggest using the analogy of a watch, which has a long heritage going back to William Paley (1743–1805). Paley asks us to imagine that a person out for a walk finds a watch and after examining its inner workings comes to the unsurprising conclusion that "the watch must have had a maker . . . who comprehended its construction, and designed its use."[18]

So, in conversation, I would say, "The world is like a watch. Just as we see the electronics of the watch working together for a beneficial purpose, so the systems of the world seem to work as well. Just as the watch was designed by an intelligent being, so is the world."

You could substitute your favorite machine or electronic device—an iPad or computer or whatever—in the analogy. I like the watch image because it comes easily to mind, due to Paley's fame in the history of philosophizing about design.

Objections to design and suggested replies. Atheists and other skeptics object to the design argument in several ways. Here are seven, along with my short replies:

1. *Believers see what they want to see.* Believers read their prior-held beliefs into nature. But, in fact, nature is simply "there," a brute fact. It's as if believers are looking at cloud formations and projecting images onto them—animals, faces, cathedrals and so forth—that aren't really there. Clouds are just clouds.

Reply. "Yes, that's possible, but it also goes the other way. Skeptics read their own theories into nature. In fact, many skeptics need to constantly remind themselves that, appearances to the contrary, there really is no designer. Why not listen to your intuition—your observations of beneficial order?" Then I would talk about a famous atheist philosopher, Antony Flew, who changed his mind after examining the complexity of the DNA molecule and came to believe in a designer.

2. *God isn't "probable."* When believers say nature seems to exhibit beneficial order and the most probable explanation of such order is God rather than nature itself, nothing has really been argued. How does one assign probabilities to God? And why is God more probable than nature? At least the mechanisms and workings of nature can be observed. God is a totally invisible and speculative explanation.

Reply. "There are many reasons to believe in God, beneficial order in nature being just one of them." This is where a cumulative case (see chapter two) for God is important. We need to be able to provide arguments for God from a variety of sources, such as history, philosophy, science and personal experience. Thus if there are already other reasons to believe in God, our observation of beneficial order in nature will be one more confirmation of an overall pattern.

3. *The multiverse theory.* The fine-tuning argument is not so impressive when one considers that there could be multiple—maybe millions—of universes out there. This "multiverse" theory greatly increases the odds of there being at least one universe that is conducive to life: this one. We won the lottery, and our presence on planet earth confirms it.

Reply. "This sounds highly speculative. What empirical evidence is there for such a theory? In any case, suppose for the moment you're right. Where did all these universes come from? What—or who—is your universe generator?" Now we are back to the cosmological argument about the origin of matter and energy (see chapter three on the grand designer). Theists will also point out that the existence of multiple universes, if real, adds even more complexity to the scenario and exhibits intelligent design all the more.

More rhetorically, I would mention that explaining the condition of the present universe by way of more universes sounds a bit desperate. Also, I'd continue to press for the incredibly low probability that, despite the possible existence of other worlds, this particular world has all the constants so finely tuned that they sustain life.[19] What are the odds? For conversation purposes, memorize and toss out one of the big numbers mentioned above from Ross or Plantinga, or just call it a zillion-to-one.

Last, I should mention that sometimes I call out my dialogue partners on their habit of invoking the phrase "It's possible that . . ." It's possible that there could be infinite universes, undiscovered scientific theories, aliens at work or alternate states of reality. This is a kind of "science of the gaps" strategy, where one has faith that science will come through in the future and plug the gaps currently occupied by superstition or ignorance—because we already know in advance (so say the opponents of design) that God cannot be an explanation.

Of course, anyone can play the possibilities game, if necessary. I can flip it around and say, in response, "It's possible that God is the explanation."

4. *The world is flawed.* This is the early Flew argument—that a perfect God would not be the cause of such an imperfect world as this. Physical defects such as cancer and other diseases, the fragile construction of the human spine, useless vestigial organs—many things about this world can be categorized as "flawed." And certainly spiritual and moral items count as well: sin, suffering, evil, billions sent to hell—how can anyone chalk this world up to the hand of a perfect, all-powerful God?

Reply. Now we are into the problem of moral and natural evil. See chapter seven and how to use the broken world image in conversation. Additionally, it is worth noting that God may have reasons unknown to us for allowing certain vulnerabilities and defects to enter the world system that he created.

5. *All design arguments can be dismissed as God-of-the-gaps strategies.* God-of-the-gaps arguments tend to plug holes ("gaps") in scientific knowledge with God. But when science eventually provides natural explanations for previously vexing questions, the believer withdraws and finds other gaps to fill with God—until those, too, are explained by science. You can see the pattern.

Reply. "I'm a big proponent of science! Sometimes Christians are accused of being anti-science in order to preserve a place for God (in the gaps of scientific knowledge), and I suppose a few are. I'm not one of them. I believe God has given science to us as a gift—a powerful 'microscope' (or telescope!) to examine and explore the creation."

Far from causing insecurity about crowding God out of the picture, the discoveries of science should help us see God in the picture. The shrinking island analogy of chapter twelve helps illuminate the relationship of God and science, suggesting that God is for, not against, scientific knowledge—and we should be as well.

Additionally, we can point out that issues such as the origin of the universe and many aspects of design argumentation are philosophical, not merely scientific.[20] Science, for example, cannot give us ultimate explanations for the existence of the world or its apparent fine-tuning. And that's where God comes in as a more comprehensive explanation.

6. Design is not real science. There is nothing about God that is observable, testable or repeatable.

Reply. This critique also applies to the multiverse theory and much of "historical science," such as theories on the origin of life and consciousness. Pretty tough to observe and perform firsthand testing on other universes or the first emergence of life on earth.

7. "The universe is not fine-tuned for humanity. Humanity is fine-tuned to the universe." This is a comment by physicist and religious skeptic Victor Stenger.[21]

Reply. But if the fine-tuning parameters were not in place, nothing of our sort of life would have arisen in the first place. Neither human life nor anything like it could ever have gotten started on its path of adaptation; it would have been shut out at the door of an "uninhabitable planet."

HOW TO TALK ABOUT DESIGN

In conversation with skeptics, I think the best overall strategy can be summarized as follows:

1. Use the royal flush and watch analogies.

2. Appeal to specific examples of fine-tuning.

3. Show yourself to be a supporter of science.

4. Continue to fall back to a cumulative-case position. This is ab-

solutely vital. The appearance of design in the universe is important by itself but not sufficient to demonstrate God's existence. Remember to play your whole orchestra, as described in chapter two.

5. Recognize that there's a certain amount of "judgment call" in design arguments. Believers and unbelievers look at the same data and come to different conclusions. As Evans and Manis note, subjective factors often come into play.[22] Yes, arguments are sound or unsound, valid or invalid. Yet the real test of an argument—especially in controversial and important issues such as design—is whether it is persuasive and to whom. When Flew converted to theism due to his marvel at the DNA molecule, he said, "[It] looked to me like the work of intelligence." "Looked to me" are the key words to notice. A judgment call.[23]

On April 8, 2010, Professor Antony Flew passed away. *The New York Times* noted that he was known to be "respectful of his opponents and driven, as he often said, by simple curiosity and a determination to go where the facts led him."[24] May that be true of both ourselves and our skeptical friends.

CHAPTER SUMMARY

In this chapter we discussed two images for design:

The royal flush. The many fine-tuning variables that combine to enable our universe to be life-permitting is like getting a royal flush a hundred times in a row. Coincidence? Not likely. Someone is messing with the cards.

The watch. When we examine or even think about a watch, we know it was designed for a purpose due to the beneficial order and purpose it exhibits. In the same way, when we see beneficial order and purpose in nature, we attribute it to a designer. This seems more reasonable than chalking it up to the blind forces of nature.

SUGGESTED RESOURCES

Lee Strobel, *The Case for a Creator: A Journalist Investigates Scientific Evidence That Points Toward God* (Grand Rapids, MI: Zondervan, 2005).

Alvin Plantinga, *Where the Conflict Really Lies: Science, Religion, and Naturalism* (New York: Oxford University Press, 2011).

Douglas Groothuis and James F. Sennett, eds., *In Defense of Natural Theology* (Downers Grove, IL: IVP Academic, 2005).

William Dembski, ed., *Mere Creation* (Downers Grove, IL: InterVarsity Press, 1998).

J. B. Stump and Alan G. Padgett, eds., *The Blackwell Companion to Science and Christianity* (West Sussex, UK: Wiley-Blackwell, 2012).

Michael Murray, ed., *Reason for the Hope Within* (Grand Rapids, MI: Eerdmans, 1993).

Hugh Ross, *The Creator and the Cosmos: How the Greatest Scientific Discoveries of the Century Reveal God,* 3rd ed. (Colorado Springs, CO: NavPress, 2011).

PART TWO

RESPONDING TO
TOUGH QUESTIONS

5

JESUS AS THE SON OF GOD

A Massive Conspiracy?

C. S. LEWIS FAMOUSLY LAID OUT FOR US three alternatives regarding the identity of Jesus Christ. Jesus was either a liar, a lunatic or the Lord: unscrupulous, crazy or the Son of God. These days, however, a fourth alternative has risen to popularity: Jesus was a legend—a legend who attained posthumous God status through the creative embellishments of his followers or maybe a legend who never existed at all, the same as Zeus or Paul Bunyan.

In short, Jesus was either a solid, real-life historical figure as the Bible recounts or a fiction. "Fiction" can be subdivided into a spectrum of views ranging from slightly to completely fictionalized.

My position is that the Jesus of Scripture was a real figure of history as recorded in the four Gospel accounts. Many times I've had the privilege of sharing this information with seekers and skeptics. Some, like Jason at Northwestern University, have been eager to hear solid support for the claim that the biblical stories of Jesus are true. Others, like my friend Lee here in the Twin Cities, adamantly oppose the stories as being false, even pernicious.

Jason had invited me to hang out in a dorm lounge one evening with a group of his friends. Not a lot of gray hair in the residence halls at NU at 10 p.m. most nights. But there I was in my favorite type of setting. Guys were sprawled around piles of junk food and libations, peppering me with questions about the credibility of the Bible.

I told them about MODEMS—not electronic communication devices, but an acronym for six reasons to trust the Jesus stories in the Bible:

Monotheism
Overlapping material
Differences
Embarrassing material
Manuscripts
Secular material

For years I'd found it difficult to organize my thoughts around the multifaceted arguments for the reliability of the Gospels. But since creating MODEMS, I can recite my case on cue, and I'd recommend the acronym to you as well.

MONOTHEISM

Many critics of the Gospels dismiss the historicity of the accounts of Jesus because of the presence of pagan mystery cults in the ancient world. These Egyptian and Hellenistic traditions feature deities and hero figures whose stories are remarkably similar, it is claimed, to those of Jesus. Isis, Osiris, Baal, Mithras and other gods and goddesses are connected to religious narratives and cultic practices that include dying and rising gods, virgin births, baptisms and blood sacrifices. Critics of the Gospels believe the early church borrowed from the vast resources of these "mysteries," as they're called, put a Jewish spin on them, and created their own god: Jesus Christ.

Evangelical scholars have given many responses. For example, they've disputed the supposed similarities between Jesus and the pagan deities, and they've questioned which way the influence actually flowed: from the mysteries to Christians or the other way around?

A third response, which is the focus of this section, is that first-century Palestinian Jews were strict monotheists (believed in only one God) and would never invent anything that could be perceived as a second "god" to go alongside Yahweh, the God of the Old Testament. Thus the Jews didn't invent Jesus. On the contrary. They discovered him in their midst, much to their surprise.

The case for Jewish monotheism rests on the idea that Jews of the time period in Palestine were resistant in certain ways to the influences of Hellenism—the pervasive Greek language and culture of Alexander the Great (356–323 B.C.) and his successors. As Hellenism spread around the Mediterranean world, so did its stock of cults and religions.

Christian scholars and others have attempted to show (successfully, in my view) that Hellenization was in some respects a thin cultural veneer on Palestinian Jewish life. In other words, Jewish culture was *painted* Greek, not *marinated* in Greek. Think of the difference: paint is superficial—it makes things look different. You can tattoo your skin, for example, and remain the same person underneath. But a marinade represents deep change. In our home when we soak chicken or beef in a marinade before grilling, it saturates the meat. So the point is that the Hellenistic "painting" of first-century Jews in Palestine didn't affect one primary area—their deeply held religious convictions, especially monotheism, which in fact they guarded closely.[1]

Hence they were not in any frame of mind to invent a divine man (Christ) but were actively resistant to the encroachments of competing religious ideas.[2] The British historian Hugh Bowden reinforces this point: "The apparent similarities [with ancient myths] mask more profound differences. In particular they give too little weight to Christianity's origins in Judaism."[3] Bowden is arguing that pagan origins for the story of Jesus Christ's life are unlikely and that if we're to look anywhere for such origins, it ought to be inside Judaism, not Greek culture.

Notice that we haven't made an actual argument for the idea that ancient Judaism guarded itself from Hellenistic religions. You can either trust Christian (and other) historians on that question or dive into the issue yourself. We are merely countering skeptics' tendency to speak overconfidently about the effects of Hellenization, thinking no one in the room will challenge their assertions. Thus you can say something like this: "I've heard that Hellenism was a pretty superficial influence on some parts of Jewish life, more like a coat of paint than a deep marinade. For example, Hellenism didn't really affect their religious beliefs, which they guarded very closely. How do you respond to that?" And then hopefully a thoughtful skeptic will take your question seriously and you can enter into a fruitful dialogue.

OVERLAPPING MATERIAL

New Testament scholar Luke Timothy Johnson makes a key point about the overlapping testimony from all the New Testament writers concerning Jesus:

> [One] historical fact is the composition of at least twenty-seven distinct compositions within a fifty year period by members of this religious movement, all of which, despite their diversity of literary genre, social setting and theological perspective, have the same Jesus as their point of focus, and the same generative matrix, namely the death and resurrection of the human person Jesus. Such highly specific historical phenomena do not arise out of generalized social conditions, psychological laws or religious types. Their necessary and sufficient cause is the death and (proclaimed) exaltation of Jesus.[4]

Johnson is referring to the remarkably unified, coherent portrait of Christ that emerges when one reads the entire New Testament. And here it should be remembered that the New Testament represents a collection of stories and letters composed by many authors, not merely a single book with a single writer. It's common to hear opponents of Christian faith pick on the small percentage of difficult passages in the Gospels and Epistles but ignore the broad unity therein. But that unity is important for establishing the true identity of Jesus.

DIFFERENCES

Continuing my late-night theological chitchat with the NU boys, I came to a place in my MODEMS presentation where there's often a great deal of misunderstanding among Christians: how differences among the Gospel accounts actually increase their credibility. It sounds counterintuitive at first, but it's a powerful argument.

To illustrate, I drew a horizontal spectrum on an easel pad, one pole labeled zero percent and the other one hundred percent. Then I asked the guys to imagine that four friends named Matthew, Mark, Luke and John attended a sporting event together and afterward each wrote down what he saw. If zero percent of the four reports harmonized with each other, we'd think the guys got their wires crossed and attended separate events. Matthew reported on horses, Mark on touchdowns, Luke and John on other sports. The credibility of the eyewitnesses would be in serious doubt.

By contrast, suppose their accounts were one hundred percent verbatim, or pretty close to it, and all four recorded an extraordinary feat: a professional baseball player hit six home runs in a single game. Most of us would be skeptical. We'd think Matthew, Mark, Luke and John huddled in a room somewhere to fabricate a single harmonized account.[5] The logic of this one hundred percent scenario seemed to connect with the NU group. I saw a few heads nod.

Christians and non-Christians alike expect the four Gospel stories to harmonize perfectly because they think that's how the Word of God should be. But in just five minutes of group discussion, most see that the one hundred percent option isn't any more believable than the zero percent option. Collusion is no better than error.

But what if the reports were in the seventy percent range, roughly speaking? What if the broad contours of the stories were pretty similar, though some of the details differed? Say Mark's account of the ball game was the shortest and most selective, Matthew's was the most focused on Jewish players, Luke's highlighted a postgame clinic for inner city kids, and John's was the most philosophical about baseball. Despite these disparate angles, the reports had much in common: The New York Yankees beat the Minnesota Twins eight to four (hugely probable, I assure you), the game was played in Minneapolis, such and such players were the stars and the goats, and so on. It seems to me we could feel pretty confident that this game actually took place and that its elements were truthful as reported by the four witnesses.

And that's just what we have in the four Gospels. They overlap a lot—I'm just calling it seventy percent for illustration purposes; don't quote me on that—and their "varying testimony," according to New Testament scholar Craig Blomberg, "will reflect the fact that the evidence consists of fragmentary excerpts from a much fuller, self-consistent body of evidence."[6] What is Blomberg saying? That there is a larger, fuller account that can be given of any event—the Christ event, in this case—and that individual reports of that event will necessarily be partial and selective. Not everything about Jesus is reported, and everything that is reported is done so from different perspectives—four Gospel perspectives, in this case. The early church selected these four "portraits" of Jesus to round out our picture of him.

Think of it: the early church knew there wasn't perfect agreement between the four accounts. They knew, for example, about the differences between the genealogies of Jesus in Matthew and Luke, about the names of the twelve disciples varying slightly in the four Gospels, and about the passion week of John's Gospel seeming different, chronologically, from the other accounts. Yet by ancient standards of precision, it's doubtful these details were of great concern. We must guard against imposing our own standards of precision onto first-century culture.[7] The early church had good reason to choose these four stories, out of all the Jesus stories written, to represent the true gospel teaching.[8]

As a result, Christian apologists note, the apparent inconsistencies between the four Gospels actually adds to their credibility. If the accounts disagreed on major topics such as the resurrection, that would be bad. If they agreed perfectly on everything, it would seem too good to be true and thus also bad. But if they represent four somewhat independent accounts of the life of Jesus from four different angles, then their credibility is solid indeed.[9]

EMBARRASSING MATERIAL

It is difficult to imagine the followers of Jesus inventing stories about him that were essentially counterproductive to their overall message. If they wished to commend the message of salvation to both Jews (at first) and Gentiles (later), why include material that would be perceived as damaging to the credibility of Jesus? But that's just what they did. A small sampling would include the people of Jesus' hometown rejecting him and limiting his ministry of miracles (Mark 6:3-6), his family thinking him "out of his mind" (Mark 3:21), his brothers not believing in him (John 7:5) and his crucifixion at the hands of Israel's sworn enemy, Rome (John 19:16)—hardly a fitting death for the long-awaited Messiah. None of this material (and much else that could be cited) makes sense as a fabrication, but only as facts of the matter.

Another category of detrimental material involves the disciples of Jesus—those who first propagated the stories about him. In the Gospel accounts they come off as foolish and obstinate. They are scolded for their lack of faith (Mark 4:40) and for fighting among themselves over who is greatest (Luke 9:46); Peter is called "Satan" for trying to prevent Jesus from going to Jerusalem to die (Mark 8:33); they fall asleep in the Garden of Gethsemane (Matthew

26:36-46); Peter promises to lay down his life for Jesus (John 13:37) only to deny him three times (John 18:17-27); the first witnesses and reporters of the empty tomb are not the slow-minded apostles but women (Matthew 28:1-10), whose testimony was generally not trusted in the ancient world.

But perhaps, the skeptic thinks, the Gospel writers should be seen as conspirators and more clever than we think. Perhaps they deliberately created flaws in the characters in order to make them appear more well-rounded and authentic. Perhaps the disciples were willing to appear foolish in the Gospel stories in order to get their evangelistic message across. But I say it stretches the limits of credulity to suppose that a first-century band of fishermen and tax collectors with little formal education could have orchestrated a scheme so thoroughly ingenious as this—and made the world believe it. More on this topic below.

MANUSCRIPTS

The fifth section of MODEMS deals with ancient manuscripts of the New Testament. The 5,700 complete or partial handwritten Greek manuscripts currently in our possession enable scholars to weed out copyist errors that crept in over the centuries and ensure that our current Bible is accurate to what was originally written. See chapter six for more detail on this important part of the argument.

SECULAR SOURCES

Quite probably I spend more time with atheists than most Christians do. I meet up with them on college campuses and carry on long-standing email dialogues with atheist friends. I read atheist books and articles and generally have a heart for them (especially the friendly ones). One thing to know about atheists is that they demand external confirmation of the story of Jesus and won't settle for internal arguments. The difference? Internal arguments are what I've been offering so far. They deal with the credibility of the early church's witness of Jesus, including the quality and reliability of ancient Christian texts. External arguments, on the other hand, would cite sources outside the church—non-Christians who wrote about the historical Jesus, especially in the first century.

The demand for external references is not unreasonable, and such evidence can be provided in limited form. What's unreasonable, in my view, is the automatic dismissal of internal sources. What's really being said is, "No one who's a true believer in X can be trusted to report the truth about X." In this case X is Christianity. So none of the apostles or other first-century followers of Jesus can really tell us anything reliable. After all, they're biased.

Of course, there's a partial truth in all this. The claims of salespeople or others with a vested interest in a cause or product should be taken with a grain of salt. But that doesn't make their claims worthless. It doesn't mean they're automatically wrong or are necessarily falsifying matters. If that were the case, the damaging material mentioned above would never have been included in the Gospel accounts. What's more, a quick dismissal of internal evidence by contemporary skeptics is also a matter of bias. Perhaps they are unfairly prejudiced against religious claims because they don't want them to be true. One time an atheist came to my home and I showed him a book containing ancient non-Christian sources regarding the life of Christ. He wouldn't even look at the book because its author was Christian.

Think of testimony from the Holocaust. Would we want to discount the "internal" stories of death camp survivors merely because they were Jews and not neutral, outside observers (if there is such a thing)? Obviously not. Jewish reports of Nazi anti-Semitism and persecution are given much credence in our culture. The same is true for victims of sexual harassment and abuse. Often a victimized woman is the only one who can tell her own tragic story and there simply is no external collaboration available—yet we are wise (and morally obligated) to take her claim seriously.

One of the criteria historians commonly use to judge ancient testimony and evidence is called "multiple attestation." It means that the credibility of historical claims increases as sources are multiplied—sources such as eyewitnesses and their associates, for example. And of course credibility dramatically increases when confirming testimony is provided by opponents or by parties with no stake in the outcome.

In conversation, then, I want to advocate for the value of internal arguments and witnesses first. I want to say to skeptics, "Don't be so quick to dismiss Christian eyewitnesses, especially if there are many voices available (multiple attestation) in the ancient world." Secondly, I want to move toward providing external evidence, which for the story of Jesus is not as impressive but is still helpful. Of the dozen or so ancient references that could be mentioned,[10] here are two of the most important:

Tacitus (c. 60–c. 120). Tacitus was a Roman historian and senator known for his careful checking of sources. In writing of the burning of Rome in A.D. 64 at the hands of the emperor Nero, he states:

> Nero set up as the culprits and punished with the utmost refinement of cruelty a class hated for their abominations, who are commonly called Christians. Christos, from whom their name is derived, was executed at the hands of the procurator Pontius Pilate in the reign of Tiberius. Checked for the moment, this pernicious superstition again broke out, not only in Judea, the source of the evil, but even in Rome.[11]

Some critics have questioned whether Tacitus can be trusted as an "external" source or whether he is writing hearsay from Christian sources. Nothing can be proven, but it stands to reason that Christian sources would have gone beyond Christ's crucifixion to mention his resurrection as well. Also, they wouldn't have referred to themselves as a "pernicious superstition." For these reasons and others we can be relatively sure of Tacitus as a reliable external source.

Josephus (37–c. 100). Josephus was a Jewish historian who mentioned Jesus twice in his writings. In *The Antiquities of the Jews* 20.9.1 we find the following passage:

> Albinus was but upon the road; so he assembled the sanhedrin of the judges, and brought before them the brother of Jesus, who was called Christ, whose name was James.[12]

Again, this is a possible external source that has been questioned by skeptics on the grounds that parts of the writings of Josephus have been modified by Christians. But this passage has withstood the criticism and stands as an important non-Christian reference to Jesus. If more were made of Jesus here—for example, lauding him as Lord or Messiah, as the early Christians were prone to do, and more were made of James, an exalted apostle—perhaps the passage would be more suspect. But this mere passing reference to Jesus seems to indicate that the text is authentic, as if Josephus is merely specifying which James and which Jesus are being referenced.

The other, longer, reference to Jesus by Josephus (*Antiquities* 18:3.3, famously called the *Testimonium Flavianum*) has admittedly been tampered with, though when the obvious Christian additions are removed, it still mentions Jesus, a "wise man" who was condemned to be crucified by Pilate.

If you're not accustomed to interacting with scholarly wrangling over historical technicalities, your eyes might be glazing over right now. My wife, Sharon, usually announces about ten minutes into one of my "fascinating" academic anecdotes that she's been hit with a headache. Still, I hope you see the importance of responding to typical skeptical assertions such as, "There is absolutely no shred of historical evidence for the life of Christ," by saying something like, "What about Tacitus and Josephus? Both are ancient non-Christian historians that mention Jesus." And if challenged by a knowledgeable skeptic, you need to go read up on Tacitus, Josephus and other non-Christian sources and then return to the dialogue. I

fear that many Christians feel so out of their element in these interactions that they simply clam up and let an often forceful skeptical voice carry the day.

Those are the six short arguments represented by MODEMS that
I presented to Jason and his NU friends. Although summarized
concisely here in print, it took a couple of hours of back-and-forth
discussion to get through the material in a live setting. Around my
bedtime of 11:30 p.m., the evening was still young in the dorm and
I was feeling surprisingly fresh. I had one last piece to add to the
presentation, after which I would need to exit directly to my
housing, as befitting my age.

A MASSIVE CONSPIRACY

The last piece is an image you can use in conversation, which we
hinted at in the "embarrassing material" section above: a massive
conspiracy.

If Jesus as portrayed in the New Testament were actually a fabrication, imagine the massive conspiratorial logistics that would have
been required to get all the New Testament writers to share the
same theological view of the Messiah and his community. Elements
included the church as the new Israel, salvation by faith through
grace, the fulfillment of the law in Jesus, the doctrine of justification, the explicit concepts of heaven and hell, Christ's disputes
with the Pharisees, his egalitarian treatment of women, the presence
and power of the Holy Spirit, a crucified and bodily risen Savior
figure who was the true Son of God and was to be worshiped
alongside the Father, and many other concepts.

And, by the way, you'd have to pull all of this off in a Roman oc-
cupation with no Internet or other technology, a serious shortage
of pen and papyrus, and excruciatingly slow travel systems—and
you'd do it in only six decades among a people group (the Jewish
community) that had been committed to the same rule of faith and
practice for more than a thousand years and were not looking for a

change such as adding a "Son" to God the Father. If this were all a fabrication, it would require a conspiratorial plot of epic proportions that I, for one, am not ready to buy.

Yet contemporary skeptics readily believe that parts or all of the Jesus stories were fictionalized by the early church. In other words, they do believe in a massive conspiracy.

Try using the phrase "massive conspiracy" with critics of the Bible, and you're likely to get a variety of responses. Some say, "Sure, it's the biggest conspiracy and power play in human history. It just shows you how gullible people are to believe so easily in superstitions."

Others, however, will spot the implications of the "massive conspiracy" analogy and perhaps soften their position. The image is effective because when a person believes in a conspiracy of this magnitude, it opens the door to belief in other conspiracies that, as a rule, would be unattractive to thoughtful skeptics.

Here's one: the Apollo moon landings conspiracy.

The whole lunar conspiracy theory goes something like this: The six Apollo moon landings of 1969–1972 were elaborate hoaxes, filmed in secret on sophisticated Hollywood-style sets and sold to the American public as historical fact. All the main players collaborated and swore themselves to secrecy—twelve astronauts, multiple NASA officials, film crews, set designers and, of course, US President Richard Nixon and other top government officials. Oh yeah—and all family members and friends of these folks as well.

Speculation on motives for such a scheme is not hard. The government wanted to (1) divert attention from the Vietnam war, (2) win the race to the moon against the Soviets, (3) save money and (4) avoid the risk of failure in space. There were other motives as well. Photos of supposed lunar scenes seem to lack stars in the background and consistent shadows from grounded objects. There's too much light here and too little there, the American flag is fluttering without the possibility of breeze, and so on.

If true, the fake moon landings would be a staggering hoax affecting the public trust and national conscience for generations. But of course many skeptics of Christianity don't believe it. They think the moon landings are true. They use internal arguments—such as the broadly unified testimony of the participants and the difficulty of covering up such a giant secret—as well as external arguments, such as confirmation from outside sources (the press, Nixon opponents and so forth) to support their beliefs. And of course I agree with them—the moon landings are not a hoax and I have no interest in siding with hoaxers or hucksters of any stripe.

How ironic that we've all joined the same team here. Many skeptics who deny the moon landing hoax on evidential grounds find a way to accept the (supposed) Jesus hoax. Perhaps they will deny that the two cases are similar due to the supernatural elements in the Gospels. But on purely historical grounds, the case for Jesus is quite strong, especially when one considers the unlikely alternative: twelve disciples and their companions created this particular Jesus—a deeply Jewish, highly complex, multilayered Messiah who turned the world on its head. Believing in a few fake moon landings seems easier by comparison.

CHAPTER SUMMARY

Remember MODEMS:

Monotheism. A good case can be made that first-century Palestinian Jews held fast to their belief in one God and would not invent a second deity—Jesus Christ.

Overlapping material. The authors of the New Testament represent multiple testimony and broad agreement about the life of Jesus.

Differences. A limited number of differences in the four Gospel accounts gives them a ring of truth. Neither zero percent agreement or one hundred percent agreement would be helpful.

Embarrassing material. The presence of material in the Gospels that places Jesus and the disciples in a potentially negative light is best explained by historical accuracy, not fiction.

Manuscripts. We have in our possession around 5,700 Greek New Testament manuscripts (in whole or in part) that enable scholars to reconstruct the original writings.

Secular material. There are around a dozen references to Jesus in non-Christian sources from the ancient world. Two mentioned above are Tacitus and Josephus.

Remember also the massive conspiracy analogy: Included in the charge that parts of Jesus' life—especially his miracles, resurrection and claims to deity—were fictionalized by his followers is that a small band of fishermen and tax collectors were somehow able to pull off the biggest hoax in human history. Six fake lunar landings filmed in a Hollywood studio and sold to the American public pales by comparison. Yet thoughtful skeptics tend to believe the Jesus conspiracy and not the lunar hoax.

SUGGESTED RESOURCES

Arthur G. Patzia, *The Making of the New Testament*, 2nd ed. (Downers Grove, IL: IVP Academic, 2011).

Paul Rhodes Eddy and Gregory A. Boyd, *The Jesus Legend: A Case for the Historical Reliability of the Synoptic Jesus Tradition* (Grand Rapids, MI: Baker Academic, 2007).

Craig L. Blomberg, *The Historical Reliability of the Gospels* (Downers Grove, IL: IVP Academic, 2007).

Craig L. Blomberg, "Jesus of Nazareth: How Historians Can Know Him and Why It Matters," in Douglas Groothuis, *Christian Apologetics: A Comprehensive Case for Biblical Faith* (Downers Grove, IL: IVP Academic, 2011).

6

THE TELEPHONE GAME

Why the Bible Is Not Full of Errors

STUMP THE CHUMP IS A FORUM on campus where students can come and pose any question they wish about Christianity in an informal, nonjudgmental setting. I am the chump. My job is to offer a thoughtful reply to students' questions and, yes, sometimes I get stumped.[1] A few topics come up repeatedly, among them the supposed corruption of the Bible as it's been "translated and retranslated over the centuries," to quote a phrase I hear often.

I remember asking one student how she knew the Bible had been tampered with and changed. Had she been adept at historical argumentation, she'd have said something like, "I just assume it has. It only makes sense that documents from the ancient world have not been preserved perfectly. So the burden of proof is on you believers." But she didn't say that. Nor do most other common folks because they have no idea about these matters. Actually, she shrugged her shoulders and mentioned she'd seen something about the history of the Bible on TV.

That level of objection to the Bible is pretty common among laypeople, though a small minority are well-informed. It's the critical professionals we need to take more seriously, and if we can understand what they're saying and craft a reply, we'll be well-prepared for everyone. Here's a sample from skeptical New Testament scholar Bart Ehrman, who can be heard these days on talk shows and other popular venues:

> Not only do we not have the originals [of the New Testament], we don't have the first copies of the originals. We don't even have copies of the copies of the originals, or copies of the copies of the copies of the originals. What we have are copies made later—much later. In most instances, they are copies made many centuries later. And these copies all differ from one another, in many thousands of places.[2]

If you're a committed Christian and you read this quote from Dr. Ehrman or hear him say it on a cable talk show, it can be a scary notion. It can shake your foundations. That can be a good thing, in my view, because many Christians breeze through life with a kind of blind faith that, if ever challenged, would crumple like a sand castle in a storm. So let's examine what Ehrman is really saying, and see how the analogy of the telephone game applies.

First, Ehrman is saying that we don't have the original copies of the books of the New Testament and in fact nothing close to it. But this isn't really earthshattering news (though sometimes it is played up that way in the media), since Christian scholars haven't claimed for hundreds of years to be in possession of the originals. Here is where modern people unfamiliar with ancient historical studies need to adjust their expectations, because there are few original manuscripts of any major author from antiquity in our possession: not Josephus, not Thucydides, not Homer, not Plato. Just to give some perspective, the earliest existing manuscript of Josephus's *Jewish Wars* is dated three to four hundred years after the original, Homer's *Iliad* nine hundred years after the original, Plato's *Tetralogies* twelve hundred years later and Thucydides' *History* thirteen hundred years after the original version.[3]

Does this mean we despair of history altogether? Not at all. Classical scholars accept the validity of many ancient texts even though the manuscript evidence is thin at times. And why not? Why think Plato didn't write Plato? Why think the thousands of quotations of Plato by other writers after his death in 347 B.C. were all false? And who would write Thucydides' *History of the Peloponnesian War* thirteen hundred years after the fact and put Thucydides' name on it—and get away with it? While many of the compositions from the time of Christ and before survive in just a few manuscript copies, the New Testament is wealthy by comparison—an embarrassment of riches, one might say, with approximately 5,700 ancient Greek manuscripts in existence.[4]

New Testament scholar Craig Blomberg puts the situation this way: "We have an unbroken sequence of ever growing textual resources (in both numbers and amount of text represented) from the early second century until the inventing of the printing press in the fifteenth century."[5] Translation: The New Testament is the bomb when it comes to the number and quality of old manuscripts in comparison with its peers. And that means we have an excellent chance of getting back to the wording of the original texts.

Second, Ehrman is saying the many manuscripts in our possession contain thousands—upwards of 400,000—copyist errors (called "variants")—"more differences among our manuscripts than there are words in the New Testament."[6] The obvious thing to remember here is that before the invention of the printing press, the books of the New Testament were copied by hand, sometimes by professional copyists with high standards, but not always. In any case copyists were prone to mistakes due to tedious work that often took place in low light conditions. They misread and miscopied words and phrases, they misspelled words, and sometimes they even changed texts due to their theological preferences. Christians holding to a high view of Scripture as inspired by God might have trouble with these facts, but there they are. However, the situation is not so dire as Ehrman suggests. Again, Blomberg:

> Overall the texts were copied with remarkable care; the vast majority of changes that were introduced involved variant spellings, the accidental omission or repetition of a single letter, the substitution of one word for another and the like. Textual critics of almost all theological stripes agree that we can reconstruct somewhere upwards of 97 percent of the New Testament text beyond a shadow of reasonable doubt. . . . All these factors set the New Testament books off from every other known work from the ancient world in terms of our ability to have confidence that we know what the original authors wrote.[7]

Even Ehrman himself acknowledges:

> The more manuscripts one discovers, the more the variant readings; but also the more the likelihood that somewhere among those variant readings one will be able to uncover the original text. Therefore, the . . . variants . . . do not detract from the integrity of the New Testament; they simply provide the data that scholars need to work on to establish the text, a text that is more amply documented than any other from the ancient world.[8]

Furthermore, nothing of real importance hangs on these "variants." Blomberg comments, "It is certainly the case that no Christian belief or doctrine depends solely on a textually disputed passage."[9] Timothy Paul Jones tells us, "More than 99 percent of the 400,000 differences fall into this category of virtually un-noticeable variants!"[10] Jones goes on to explain that the task of scholars is to compare copies of the manuscripts with each other in order to determine which is closest to the original. This method is especially effective when one remembers that the work of copying was carried out in diverse places during a period of fourteen hundred years. Thus sources are numerous and varied for recapturing original wordings.[11]

THE TELEPHONE GAME ANALOGY

The general public and especially skeptics tend to think of the history of the Bible (and here we are focusing on the New Testament) as a linear process that began with the pure original compositions, then was changed and corrupted bit by bit, whether due to error or deliberate tampering, down through the centuries, until what we have today is a totally corrupted text. Some even think that every new translation of the Bible throughout history is merely based on the previous translation and nothing else—and so strays even further from the original—which is a bizarre and mistaken belief. Either way, the "telephone game" is often cited to make the point. The game begins with one person whispering a phrase into a neighbor's ear, who then whispers the phrase to the next person, and so on around the circle until the last person receives the phrase and proclaims it aloud, often with hilarious results.

So let's begin with the phrase "I ate toast this morning." After a transmission or two it becomes "I hate toast," and then "I hate the coast," then on and on until the final person announces, "I hate the coast and I am in mourning." On the surface this process sounds like a plausible explanation for the faulty transmission of ancient texts down through the centuries, but here is where I step into the analogy and turn it on itself: there are actually several circles that all begin with the same phrase. So whenever there is doubt about the original phrase, I don't just compare the final results of each circle, I go back to the second and third individuals in each circle and find out what they heard. Quite simply, I check out an earlier version of the story to ensure accuracy. I cross-compare.

And that's pretty much what New Testament scholars do. When they find differences in thirteenth-century texts, for example, they check earlier texts to head off mistakes. And if one knows from what part of the world a text originated, chances are that most or all of the texts from that region have the same mistake, which can then be eliminated. Additionally, an obvious advantage of the history of Bible transmission over the telephone game is that the Bible comes to us in print, while the telephone game is an oral exercise. Cross-comparing the written word is much more reliable than doing so with the spoken word.

PRINCIPLES FOR CHOOSING TEXTS

Timothy Paul Jones, a veteran translator of ancient texts, provides eight principles for choosing the best texts when there are problems, of which I will mention three: age, geography and length.[12] That is, when forced to choose one reading over another, look for the oldest, most geographically diverse, shortest option. Usually, an older version is more reliable. So is a reading that is found in diverse places geographically. Shorter is generally more reliable because scribes tended to add rather than delete material. Back to the telephone game: earlier in the circle is more reliable, as are common wording from diverse circles (different circles playing the same game in separate rooms, say) and shorter phrases (people tend to add words as the game progresses).

So when someone tosses a comment out there about the Bible being corrupted through copying and translating through the centuries, ask how they know that's true. And if they bring up the telephone game analogy, turn it in on itself and point out that scholars have access to more than just one circle and can also check sources earlier in each circle. If the telephone game is not brought up, bring it up yourself. Say, "A lot of people think this process of copying the Bible is like a single circle of people playing the telephone game. But in reality, there are many circles playing the game, and scholars can compare the circles in order to recover the original phrase." Then expand on that if you wish with Jones's three criteria. Better yet, read Jones's excellent little book for yourself, which is written for laypeople: *Misquoting Truth: A Guide to the Fallacies of Bart Ehrman's* Misquoting Jesus.

SUGGESTED RESOURCES

Timothy Paul Jones, *Misquoting Truth: A Guide to the Fallacies of Bart Ehrman's* Misquoting Jesus (Downers Grove, IL: IVP Academic, 2007).

Craig L. Blomberg, "Jesus of Nazareth: How Historians Can Know Him and Why It Matters," in Douglas Groothuis, *Christian Apologetics: A Comprehensive Case for Biblical Faith* (Downers Grove, IL: IVP Academic, 2011).

Craig A. Evans, *Fabricating Jesus: How Modern Scholars Distort the Gospels* (Downers Grove, IL: IVP Books, 2008).

7

BROKEN WORLD

And Other Images for the Problem of Suffering and Evil

AT A UNIVERSITY IN THE MIDWEST, a rather unique young man once asked me for an appointment, and since it's pretty much my job to talk with college students (and he intrigued me), I agreed. At the appointed time I showed up and followed him to an elevator in the student union. The enclosed space felt crowded as we descended to the building's lower level. When the lift hit bottom, the doors parted and he made his way purposely down one narrow hallway, then another, to the campus radio station, nearly losing me in the process. I accelerated to keep pace. At the entrance he turned and gave a smirk, then dug in his pockets for an illicit key and let us in. He motioned to a chair and I sat down, feeling a little unbalanced while taking in the dimly lit surroundings. I'd have been totally cool in a generic classroom or science lab or dorm lounge, but covert ops in a darkened underground studio had me on edge.

Facing him uneasily, I noticed that my eyes were elevated above his by about six inches. I guess that was to be expected, though, seeing as how he was in a wheelchair.

Steve was refreshingly blunt. Alcoholic father, confinement to a chair, the stabbing pain of losing two friends to suicide—Steve was falling into atheistic objections to faith. But the "carrier" of these objections was not primarily intellect; it was his own personal experience of hell—that is, the absence of God. He'd prayed his guts out, he'd cried to heaven, he'd "sought" the kingdom of God as the Scripture directs, but he'd received nothing. He didn't feel God at all, just empty space all around. And so, lacking any visceral confirmation of God's being there when needed most, the philosophical objections to God's existence he'd dismissed for so many years seemed more valid than before.

Steve tried a few out on me, which I'll paraphrase: If God is supposedly loving and caring, why don't I feel his love? Why has he abandoned me at the lowest point of my life? Apparently, he's the God of good times but when the going gets tough he vanishes. And if God is supposedly all-powerful as the Bible teaches, why doesn't he just snap his fingers and get me out of this damn chair? How much work would it be for God to simply say the word and give me a happy, normal life? Maybe the real answer is not so much that God is uncaring or unwilling to act, maybe it's that he doesn't exist at all. Maybe he's imaginary.

I have to admit, for a moment I was inclined to agree. Who can make a more compelling argument for God's absence than a suffering person? And beginning with God's perceived absence, isn't it a fairly short step to arrive at God's nonexistence?

One reason Steve was so challenging is that his case required two different kinds of response from me: pastoral and philosophical. Quite often it's one or the other; rarely is it both. Most hurting people aren't looking for theological and philosophical answers—they just want to be cared for. So if we are sensitive to such situations we will give empathy from our hearts. But Steve was pushing on the philosophical end of things as well, testing my ministerial dexterity.

I told Steve that we live in a broken world. This is an image that is helpful in a variety of subtopics within the problem of suffering and evil. Why are babies born with birth defects? Broken world. Why did my dad die of cancer in 1991? Broken world. Why does a student experience unwanted same-sex attraction? Broken world. Why did a 2004 tsunami kill a quarter-million people? You know my answer.

Theologian Cornelius Plantinga uses the phrase "not the way it's supposed to be" to get at the same idea.[1] The world is malfunctioning. Things don't work right. There's "not supposed to be" crime, hate, violence, injustice, racism, lying, cheating, disease and natural disasters. We know something is wrong; it's all supposed to be different. This can't be what God intended.

Why is the world broken? Because we broke it. That's the story of the Fall as recorded in Genesis 3. Part of God's response to the defection of Adam and Eve was that the ground itself would be cursed and would yield its fruit only through hard labor (Genesis 3:17-18). The apostle Paul picks up the theme in Romans 8:19-22 when he tells us that the creation was "subjected to frustration," is in "bondage to decay," and has been "groaning as in the pains of childbirth," waiting for its liberation.

Thus we experience brokenness in many different ways. Our bodies let us down, relationships are in shambles, cultures clash, the environment is hostile and, most pointedly, we lose control of our own internal motivations and desires. To be sure, there is good as well: in each area God's grace is evident. Still, it's difficult to escape the conclusion that the world as we experience it is not supposed to look this way.

The harm we inflict on one another is what philosophers call "moral evil." And the brokenness of creation is called "natural evil," which is the category of disease, earthquakes, killer storms, wildfires and other natural phenomena that cause so much pain. It's helpful to remember that natural evil was tied to moral evil from the very onset of the Fall—that is, when we fell away from God we took the world down with us.

But if God is loving and all-powerful, why would he let the Fall happen in the first place? Why create a world in which moral and natural evil are even possible? Shouldn't a perfect God create a perfect world?

A LOVING, ALL-POWERFUL GOD SHOULDN'T ALLOW EVIL (PART 1): THE ROBOT ANALOGY

Today's university students have a strong concern for the principle of fairness. Many insist it's not fair of God to create a world he knows will go bad, in which billions of people in history will experience significant suffering and billions will be consigned to hell for their lack of faith. If God were really "God," he'd have created a world without suffering and evil or kept his creating to himself.

In response to this idea of God creating a more perfect world (or not creating at all), theologians have developed a powerful argument called the "free will defense." Essentially, it says that God created human beings for the purpose of living in a loving relationship with himself and with each other. But in order for these relationships to be authentic, he endowed us with free will. He didn't create robots programmed with a "love chip," he created free creatures in his own image who could love (or not) of their own volition.[2] God valued a world of freedom more than he valued a world of robots—or no world at all.

Unfortunately, human beings chose to reject God and the beautiful life he had given them. They exercised their free will, as just described, for ill. Thus when critics blame God for the presence of suffering and evil, the free will defense argues that we are to blame. We are the free agents who caused both moral and natural evil by divorcing ourselves from God.

The point was pressed on me a step further one afternoon in a dining hall at Case Western Reserve University in Ohio. Miguel was a grad student and atheist in his beliefs. He countered my robot analogy by shining the spotlight of blame back on the source of everything: God. "Wasn't it God," he insisted, "who set up the initial conditions of the creation that made sin possible? Therefore, God is ultimately responsible."

I responded by saying that God created human beings to develop us into his agents of hope and love in a broken world, empowered by his Spirit. It's easy to look back on humanity's choice to "go bad" and, yes, unfortunately that's what we've done as a race. But the invitation to "do good" as his image-bearing representatives is also there—which opens the door to a life of fulfillment in personal relationship to God. And this brought me right back to the analogy at hand: human beings, not robots, are able to fulfill this double calling of friendship with God and service to a hurting world.

Miguel seemed somewhat satisfied with my reply—not that I directly and fully resolved his question. But on this issue, inviting his attention to the very real potential for good in a broken world proved helpful. Even so, the grad student had an additional challenge for my consideration, to which I'll return below under the remote control analogy.

A LOVING, ALL-POWERFUL GOD SHOULDN'T ALLOW EVIL (PART 2): THE PERSEVERING PARENT

For readers who find the analogy of the robot troubling due to its affirmation of human free will that conflicts (so it seems) with God's sovereignty,[3] I offer the image of the persevering parent. Imagine a parent who permits a son or daughter to fall into trouble of some sort so that a greater purpose will be served in the long run. A grieving but brave mother told me recently of her twenty-something son who had fallen into drug use and could not pay his rent. After attempting to get him into therapy and bailing him out of several jams, she released him to his habits. He was sleeping in his car in the frigid temperatures of Wisconsin. Heartbroken over her wayward son and his suffering, she still refused to give him money or coerce his obedience. She permitted him to live in humiliation and hardship for a greater purpose down the road—namely, that he would of his own accord come to his senses and return to his family. This is precisely the story of the Prodigal Son of Luke 15:11-32.

In regard to the Fall recorded in Genesis 3, we may say that a loving, all-powerful God allowed humanity to fall into sin for what philosopher Paul Helm calls "the highest and holiest reasons even though the detail of such reasons may be at present hidden from us."[4] It wouldn't be accurate to say that God caused the Fall, for he cannot do evil, yet he permitted it. We are left to trust in his mercy, love and justice that this human-divine separation will eventually fulfill God's purposes more perfectly than any other course of events.

Remember this image, then: God is the persevering parent who, out of love for his image bearers, allowed humanity to go astray for a greater good—though we may not be privy to the exact nature of that good. You may also remember the courageous mother who permitted her son to fall into harm's way (sleeping in his car) with the intent of reshaping his character for the rest of his life.

IF GOD IS SOVEREIGN, HUMAN FREEDOM IS A FICTION: THE REMOTE CONTROL ANALOGY

Back to the dining hall at Case Western. Miguel pointed out to me that if God knows the future, then he knows the free choices human beings will make. And what God knows in advance must happen, for God cannot hold false beliefs. So perhaps our belief in human freedom is a convenient fiction designed to get God off the hook for the presence of evil in the world.

Sipping my Diet Pepsi to stall for time, I wondered to myself what sort of IQ juice the young atheist was drinking.

I noted that from a Christian perspective there's a difference between God observing an event and God causing an event to happen. Imagine that God is holding a remote control for the universe. He can push a button and "make happen" whatever he wants. But out of respect for human free will, he merely watches the big screen and refrains from using the remote to forcibly change the script. That's not to say he is idle and passive. On the contrary, the Scriptures are full of references to the activity of God in the universe. The specific point of the remote control analogy, however, is to show that just because God truly knows a given event in advance doesn't mean he is the direct cause of that event. Just because he has foreknowledge of a plane crash, for instance, doesn't mean he caused it to occur.

To my surprise, once again Miguel nodded his approval. Unfortunately, he had many other objections to Christian faith that prevented him from embracing Jesus. But on this day, perhaps one or two barriers to faith were removed.

WHO'S RESPONSIBLE FOR SUFFERING AND EVIL? THE DYSFUNCTIONAL FAMILY ANALOGY

We move from the free will defense and a good God permitting evil to a more relational analogy for human participation in sin. This analogy can be helpful in evangelistic conversations, especially if you and your dialogue partner are not oriented toward philosophy. It's the dysfunctional family analogy.

Through no fault of their own, children are born into dysfunctional families. They grow up in households that are characterized by irresponsible behaviors such as abuse and neglect. Love itself may be virtually absent. None of this is their doing, of course, until they become active participants in the problem. At some point they begin to make their own negative contributions to the family, bringing harm to the lives of others—"hurt people hurt people." So while the "system" itself is not the fault of a child, his or her sinful contributions to the system certainly are the individual's fault and thus blameworthy.

The dysfunctional family is a great analogy for sin because it recognizes that after the Fall, all humans are born into a broken system they did not directly cause. The sin of the world is not their fault, per se. But early in life they begin making their own contribution to the sinful condition of humankind, and for this each person is responsible before God.

WHY IS GOD SILENT IN THE FACE OF SUFFERING AND EVIL? THE BIG STORY

In chapter six I discussed the outreach event I do on college campuses called "Stump the Chump," a safe forum where students gather to ask questions about Christianity and I try to offer a considered reply. Rarely does a whole session go by without someone raising the question of why God seems so passive in the face of suffering and evil. Sometimes it's personal: Does God even care about my mother's brain tumor? If so, why doesn't he heal her?

Before diving into any theological speculation about such a matter, it's important for me to show true compassion for this hurting person and to model that for those gathered. More often, however, students raise questions on the macro level: Why did God allow an earthquake to occur that took tens of thousands of innocent lives? Where was God in the Holocaust? In response, I almost always tell what I call the "Big Story." I've chopped it up into bite-sized points below. In the telling, of course, it all flows together. Here goes:

1. Father, Son and Holy Spirit are (and were) united in eternal love relations. That's the nature of their relationship in eternity (Mark 1:9-11; John 14:25-26; 17:20-23).

2. Their love spilled over into the creative act of making the universe. "God so loved the world . . ." (John 3:16).

3. God made human beings in his image to love him back of their own accord, but they refused and fell away, taking the creation down with them, resulting in a broken world (Genesis 3).

4. So why didn't God send his Son to die for the sins of the world five minutes after Adam and Eve fell away? Because he allows the dreadful consequences of sin to play themselves out for mil-

lennia in our timeline. He is the persevering parent. When we turned our back on him, he allowed us to indulge ourselves. He released his hand. Part of the judgment on sin is that God gives us over to our sin (Romans 1:24-31).

5. God is unsatisfied with this "great divorce," so he works to restore the world to himself, gradually and slowly. He is patient with the process. He doesn't just snap his fingers and make everything better. He's not a genie. Were he to eliminate all sin instantaneously, none of us would survive. Rather, he works a little at a time: choosing a people for himself (Israel), providing the law and the prophets and, when the time was right, sending his Son as the ultimate solution for sin. So his forbearance and gradual redemptive process is really an act of mercy and love toward us (Romans 3:21-26).

6. Jesus shows himself a fellow sufferer—one who empathizes with our pain—as he dies on a cross for our sins and overcomes death through his resurrection. All who place their faith in Jesus will experience a restored relationship with God and will receive the gift of eternal life (Hebrews 2:9-17; John 3:16).

7. God is more interested in our character than our comfort. He allows trials in our lives to shape us into the kind of people he originally envisioned (1 Peter 1:7).

8. In response to the prayers of his people, God acts directly at times with miracles of healing, but not always. What he does promise in every single circumstance is his presence. As a fellow sufferer, God draws near to us in our own suffering (2 Corinthians 1:3-5).

9. Sometimes we as Christians are guilty of sitting in the ivory tower, wondering why God doesn't stop evil and relieve suffering, when we should be out there in the trenches acting as God's hands and feet to minister to a hurting world (Ephesians 2:10).

Creating Your Own Big Story

Depending on the situation, there are different versions of the
Big Story that I use. Sometimes I summarize it in thirty seconds
or less. In extended conversation I can stretch it out and support it with detail for hours. The version scripted above takes
me about five minutes to explain. As an exercise, practice explaining the Big Story to a friend. Develop versions that take one,
five, ten and twenty minutes to explain. In longer versions you
can insert parts of your own story of turning away from God but
then receiving his love and mercy through Jesus.

There are several benefits to laying out this Big Story. First, the
story provides an overall grid for handling most individual questions on the topic of suffering and evil, and it enables you to be
consistent in your replies. For example, on the question of why
God often seems passive and silent in the face of suffering, the Big
Story reminds us that God allows the consequences of human disobedience to unfold naturally, resulting in experiences of emotional
and physical pain.

Such trials in our lives are helpful for character building (see
point seven above), to the point where the book of James exhorts,
"Consider it pure joy, my brothers and sisters, whenever you face
trials of many kinds, because you know that the testing of your faith
produces perseverance. Let perseverance finish its work so that you
may be mature and complete, not lacking anything" (James 1:2-4).
So while the Big Story itself doesn't contain all this detail, it provides
an initial framework for discussing the subject of God's passivity
and, of course, a variety of other topics related to suffering and evil.

Second, the Big Story shows seekers and skeptics a snapshot of
an alternative universe called Christianity that addresses suffering
and evil directly without sidestepping issues. That doesn't mean
Christians have easy answers to anything. In fact, we should be the

first to admit that the coexistence of a good God and evil is an extremely difficult combination to accept. The Big Story, however, offers plausible explanations for things inside a narrative framework. It helps critics see how Christians handle the problem of suffering and evil overall.

A third benefit of telling (and retelling) the Big Story is that it enables you, the witness to Christ, to remember your lines. I'm being practical here. Most folks have trouble rehearsing abstract arguments for God, such as the free will defense or a variety of technical issues I haven't mentioned such as soul-building arguments, first-order evils, second-order goods and the like. Indeed, I do this for a living and sometimes I can't come up with that stuff on the fly. But I can always remember the Big Story—and so can you.

Finally, the Big Story grounds your side of the conversation in the Bible. Never forget the obvious: You're speaking from a Christian point of view, which means you're actually "teaching the Bible" to seekers and skeptics. You're laying it out there as thoughtfully and persuasively as you can, but really, it's God's job to take your words and apply them to the heart and mind of the other person. You're just the conduit. That's no excuse to be sloppy or otherwise unprepared, but it does place the responsibility for positive results in the right hands.

DOESN'T GOD CARE? THE SUFFERING CHRIST

When I was in my thirties and my dad was being attacked by cancer, I felt stupid. I was never able to come up with those inspiring little speeches you see on TV or the movies that really hit home for a suffering person. Nor was I able to drop the punchy one-liner that would be truly memorable to him. He lived in Florida, I in Minnesota. During his final months his personality gradually shut down, which made our occasional phone calls feel pretty hollow.

I flew to Naples to visit him. He'd been a public figure his whole life, in the music and entertainment business, as was I, in ministry.

I told him how much I'd learned from him over the years and how I tried to emulate his ways. Then I said something about his sad condition that finally seemed to matter after so many faltering attempts: Jesus, too, was a sufferer. His death on the cross was a demonstration of how much God cares for us. That was about it. I saw him nod and take it in.

I remember offering a prayer at Dad's memorial service for all those gathered to mourn his passing. Standing on the platform, I squeezed my eyes shut and settled my body into the position of an imagined crucifix, arms extended maximally, and prayed, "Lord Jesus, receive my dad into your outstretched arms, arms that hung on a tree, arms that accept forgiven sinners into your holy presence. Amen."

Maybe I'm just stating the obvious when I say that the fact of the torn body of Jesus is the ultimate image of God's love for us and his empathy for our condition. From incarnation to termination God was—and is—truly with us. His mercies are ever new and everlasting.

CHAPTER SUMMARY

Objection or Question	Image to Use
Why is there suffering and evil?	Broken world: The world is in a state of brokenness because when we fell away from God, we broke it. Thus we live in constant danger of harm from other people (moral evil) and nature (natural evil such as hurricanes and floods).
A loving, all-powerful God shouldn't allow evil (part one).	The robot analogy: God loves us and created us in his image to return that love freely, of our own accord, rather than creating us as robots, programmed to love. Unfortunately we used our free will to turn our back on God and fall into evil.
A loving, all-powerful God shouldn't allow evil (part two).	The persevering parent: Just like a loving parent who allows her son or daughter to go through hard times to learn certain lessons and achieve a greater good, God permitted humanity to fall into sin. Being finite beings, we do not share God's perspective on the world and will not know all his reasons and plans. But we can trust in his good character to do what is best for humanity.

Objection or Question	Image to Use
Because of God's sovereignty, human freedom is a fiction.	The remote control: God can observe events in the future without causing them to happen. It's as if God is watching a preview of time on a big screen TV without using the remote control to program the events.
Who's responsible for suffering and evil?	The dysfunctional family analogy: A human being entering the world is analogous to a child being born into a dysfunctional family. Both inherit a broken system for which they are not responsible. Yet at some point each makes sinful contributions to the system for which they are blameworthy. Responsibility for evil, then, rests with the "family" as a whole, as well as with each family member.
Why is God silent in the face of suffering and evil?	The Big Story: This begins with a loving God who creates free beings who fall away from him, taking the world down with them. God allows the consequences of the fall to play out in the human drama, resulting in broken people living in a broken world. Very gradually, God restores the world to himself but almost never snaps his fingers to make things better instantly. When the time was ripe, and because of his love and mercy, he sent his Son into the world as a fellow sufferer who empathizes with our own suffering. He dies for sins and overcomes death, receiving into eternal life all those who place their faith in him. Yet on this side of heaven, we continue to experience the pain and cruelty of a broken world.
Doesn't God care?	The suffering Christ: This isn't really an analogy, just a striking image: Jesus hangs on a cross, absorbing all the sin of the world into his body. He never stayed above the fray, never remained high and dry. Rather he came into the world to identify with his beloved creatures in a radical way. He showed his love and care by subjecting himself to the excruciating pain and humiliation of dying on a cross for our sins.

SUGGESTED RESOURCES

Cornelius Plantinga, *Not the Way It's Supposed to Be: A Breviary of Sin* (Grand Rapids, MI: Eerdmans, 1995).

C. Stephen Evans and R. Zachary Manis, *Philosophy of Religion: Thinking About Faith*, 2nd ed. (Downers Grove, IL: IVP Academic, 2009), chap. 7.

James K. Beilby and Paul R. Eddy, eds., *Divine Foreknowledge: Four Views* (Downers Grove, IL: IVP Academic, 2001).

William L. Rowe and William J. Wainwright, *Philosophy of Religion: Selected Readings,* 3rd ed. (New York: Oxford University Press, 1998), part 3.

Peter Kreeft and Ronald Tacelli, *Handbook of Christian Apologetics* (Downers Grove, IL: InterVarsity Press, 1994), chap. 6.

8

CHRISTIANS BEHAVING BADLY

Don't Blame the Hammer

WHEN I TALK ON COLLEGE CAMPUSES about hypocrisy and the church, I ask students to share an incident from their hometown or that they've heard about recently in the media that involved "Christians behaving badly," that is, hypocrisy in the church. Just to stimulate their thinking, I mention a few categories such as clergy sex scandals, financial fraud, racial slurs and homophobia.

Students never have any trouble coming up with their own material.

After several minutes of depressing discussion, I ask everyone to imagine they could be God for a day. One single day. In their position as deity, what would they do about the many sins of the church?

"Nuke 'em" is a pretty common response, as is "throw down lightning bolts" and "I'd clean house. Now."

There's a lot of anger out there directed at the church for the way it behaves—or is perceived to behave. And what separates the sins of the church from the sins of everyone else is that Christians are supposed to know better. Christians are the ones who call for moral reform in society, who often style themselves as holy and righteous saints, looking down upon the vices of others. They're known for condemning things such as prayerlessness in schools, abortion and

the teaching of evolution, but often fail to observe sexual boundaries and financial laws themselves.

Historically speaking, there is plenty of material to make a
Christian blush. The church directly carried out or was significantly involved in the Crusades, various Inquisitions and the
Salem witch hunts. Critics also point to Christian "dominion," a
doctrinal impulse derived from the Genesis account of creation,
as the driving force behind the whole project of Western imperialism. It's what sent the European fleets around the globe to col-
onize the heathen and educate the savages and force human
nature into civility as defined by a small group of nations. The
same Bible that teaches the love of Jesus apparently also teaches,
or at least allows, the subjugation of women, the oppression of
ten million African slaves and the forced removal of hundreds of
thousands of Native Americans from their territories to be imprisoned on reservations.

The church is supposed to "walk the talk" and "practice what it
preaches," but the perception among academics (against Western
hegemony and patriarchy) and common folk alike (hurt by a church
leader and never going back to church) is that hypocrisy in the
church essentially destroys its credibility as an institution and casts
serious doubt on its claim that God even exists, let alone that he "sent
Jesus to die for sins" as the exclusive way of salvation. One strident
atheist I met with recently summed it up well: "I'm angry! The
church is wrecking our nation and I plan to do something about it."

A CAREFUL CHRISTIAN RESPONSE

In live conversations, the first thing I want to say in response to
such charges is that yes, there's a lot of truth there. No need for me
to get defensive. God willing, there will be time later to ask a critic
to consider additional factors, such as Christianity's positive contributions to society and whether it's always "true Christians" who
do the damage. But for the moment I want to stand up and humbly

confess our faults. We Christ followers should be good at that.

One Sunday morning at Grace Church Roseville I watched my pastor, Jason Stonehouse, model this posture of humility. He started off a sermon on the topic of sexuality by apologizing for how the church has treated gay people. I remember the five-second silence of eternity that ensued. He said, "I'm sorry," then there was nothing. He stood there and absorbed the array of reactions that filled the silent auditorium as the implications of his words sank in. Have you ever been in a place where emotion was as tangible as any material object, though audibly you heard not a sound? This was it.

I suppose a few folks objected to this show of remorse. But most members of our congregation are sensitive to gay friends and acquaintances who've felt the sting of inhospitality or even outright condemnation from Christians. Thus they appreciated our pastor's words, which modeled for them the kind of humility that helps soften the accusation of hypocrisy.

After his public confession, Pastor Jason went on to lay out the Bible's teaching on sexuality—with no apology. And that brings us to the next step in our response to critics.

DON'T BLAME THE HAMMER

Once I have sincerely acknowledged harm done in the name of Christ, I can begin to whittle away the untruthful and misguided parts of the accusations of hypocrisy, being careful not to suddenly "take back" anything I've just confessed or to be evasive in any way. Here is an image I often use: Don't blame the hammer. Meaning, if I pound dents in your car with a hammer, do you blame the hammer? Of course not. The hammer is merely a tool. Blame the person—blame me—not the hammer. Dude, the hammer is not the problem!

In the same way, when flawed human beings use religion to harm others, blame the human beings, not religion. We don't apologize for God; we just say that things get twisted at times to sinful purposes by sinful people. A pretty simple argument.

Additionally, the hammer image sets up several avenues of fruitful conversation: imposters who misuse the hammer, redemptive ways to use the hammer, and parallels to the hammer.

Imposters who misuse the hammer. One of my favorite outreach events we've done at Macalester College was on the topic of Christianity and Western imperialism. We invited Dr. Terry LeBlanc, a committed Christian and a leader in the Native American community, to serve on a panel with a Macalester anthropology professor. Both scholars did a good job presenting the many social and personal ills that resulted from the advance of European armies and culture across the Atlantic Ocean into North America. Native Americans, sometimes called "First Nations" peoples or simply "First Peoples," were brutalized and lied to. Native kids were removed from their families and placed in schools of religious and cultural indoctrination, where many endured sexual abuse from clergy and volunteers. I myself have visited the Pine Ridge Indian Reservation in South Dakota several times, so I was feeling the heat of this litany of harm being reeled off by our panelists as I thought of the brokenness I'd witnessed on the reservation.

At one point, however, the conversation took a stunning turn: Dr. LeBlanc told of the wonderful gospel message coming to his family and tribe through the gentle persistence of godly missionaries. Probably at this point a few in the audience checked out, mentally. Yet a First Nations PhD is precisely the person to make such a statement. Then he went further, and this is the part I'd been waiting to hear, the part that pertains most closely to the hammer image: Not everyone who marches in the name of God is a true follower of Jesus.

It seems a simple point, doesn't it? Posers are everywhere. They are the phishers of religion, spamming the world with false messages about Christ and the church. Just because I wield the hammer of God when I put dents in your car doesn't make me a true follower of Jesus. And just because the "dominion" impulse of Judeo-Christian European civilization was corrupted into centuries of colonial aggression doesn't mean that kings and queens and commanders of soldiers were Christians in the biblical sense of that word.

And what is a Christian? What is a Christ follower? The answer is straightforward: someone who follows Christ with his or her life. You should be able to tell something about the followers by looking at the leader, but it seems to me that the Jesus of Scripture would never enslave Africans or destroy First Nations people or act as the aggressor to begin war. And therefore many of those who carried out such pogroms were not really his. They did not actually belong to Jesus.

It's true that some of the perpetrators were, in fact, true Christians who misused their power, and for those we must take responsibility. They represent our heritage, our community. We are connected to them, even if somewhat indirectly, and for their actions I apologize.

But the imposters? The ones who wreak havoc in the name of God without bothering to even know and love God? The soldiers of hate and destruction who wield the hammer of religion, pounding down on the heads of the innocent? The Ku Klux Klan, for instance? No. We must reject the charge of hypocrisy against the church when the parties in question—by standards of the New Testament—are not the true church. This is a point to make to critics.

In order to crystallize, conversationally, the idea of rejecting "imposter" Christians, try the image of "imposter cops." Let's say a couple of bad guys decide to impersonate police officers. They show up at your front door wearing official-looking uniforms. They flash badges, enter your home, tie you up and rob you blind. Who's to blame for this crime? Real cops? Obviously not. The whole institution of law enforcement? Surely, no! Similarly, it's unreasonable to blame the church for its pretenders.

The question may arise at this point of how we know whether a perpetrator is a true Christian. This can get sticky, and since my main focus here is conversational images rather than spiritual discernment, I offer a practical reply: just say you don't always know. But then neither does your critic, right? The person bringing the charge of hypocrisy doesn't necessarily know whether the guilty party is authentically Christian or a phony. So if there is doubt, you can press the point. You can ask, "How do you know if that person is a true believer in Jesus? If he is, then I'm sorry. But if he isn't, your criticism hardly applies to Christianity."

Who's Responsible?

Why apologize for what others have done? Why as a twenty-first-century Christian should I apologize for twelfth-century Crusaders or eighteenth-century slave owners? Even if they were true Christians, I wasn't there. I'm not responsible.

Reply: If we hold to a strong view of the body of Christ, we will see ourselves as spiritually connected to Christians of all times and places. Through Jesus' suffering, we are "blood relations" with the saints through the ages. Thus we identify with them radically. Think of Daniel or Nehemiah who offered prayers of confession to God on behalf of the people even though they themselves didn't necessarily participate directly in the offenses—especially those of prior time periods (see Daniel 9:5-15 and Nehemiah 1:6-7).

This view of interconnectedness is rare. Not many atheists are apologizing for their fellow "atheists behaving badly" in twentieth-century communist regimes. But Christians are different. We can stand out from the crowd by taking at least some level of responsibility for the actions of fellow believers.

Redemptive ways to use the hammer. Once you have put the hammer image into play in an apologetic conversation or presentation and perhaps dealt with the issue of imposters as discussed above, you can begin providing examples of redemptive usage. My favorite one is this: "There is actually a right use of the hammer, and it happens all the time! The right use of the hammer is to 'pound nails' to serve other people, such as with Habitat for Humanity."

In other words, focus on the good that religion has done in society. I often mention the many food and clothing shelves supported by churches in my community, or the "Extend Grace" days that my church in Roseville, Minnesota, sponsors, where Christian volunteers go into the city to serve in social agencies in the name of Christ. As a matter of fact, there are so many Christian justice and relief organizations operating these days, we can hardly think of them all. Just mention International Justice Mission or World Vision or Catholic Charities or Lutheran Social Services or Midwest Challenge (or an agency in your town or neighborhood), and you've said something about proper use of the hammer. Here are three examples of redemptive hammer usage:

1. *Habitat for Humanity.* Habitat is an ideal hammer application because its business is construction. Memorizing a few facts helps drive home the point. Did you know that Habitat was founded in 1976 as a Christian organization and its mission is still based on Christian principles? And did you know that Habitat has built more than 500,000 homes and served 2.5 million low-income people worldwide using mostly volunteer labor? Now that's a proper use of the hammer!

2. *Christian hospitals and the Red Cross.* Due to many passages in the New Testament that call the church to the work of healing and caregiving—and that tell of Christ modeling such ministries (a few examples are Matthew 25:41-45; Luke 9:2; 1 Corinthians 12:9; James 5:14-15)—the early Christians brought the sick and dying into their homes. Pagan cultures in the Roman Empire, by contrast, often shunned the weak and sickly and had few if any care facilities

for civilians. Christian hospitals were established throughout Europe from the fourth century on. By the fifteenth century, 37,000 Benedictine Monasteries cared for the sick.

Florence Nightingale, a committed Christian of nineteenth-century England, spearheaded a revolution in nursing. And in the United States, church-sponsored hospitals bearing names such as Lutheran, Baptist and Methodist sprang up around the country after the Civil War, many of which remain to the present day.

The Red Cross was founded in Geneva in 1864 by a Christian humanitarian, Henry Dunant, who was deeply moved in Italy by witnessing bloody battles and neglect of the wounded. In 1901 he received the first-ever Nobel Prize for his work.[1] Clara Barton, another committed Christian, helped bring the Red Cross to the United States after risking her life many times in the service of wounded soldiers during the Civil War.

It's no exaggeration to say that Christian people and Christian principles were the major influence of health care in Western civilization from the first through the mid-twentieth centuries.[2] Thus in conversation I can say to a skeptic, "I realize that Christian history is far from perfect. Terrible things have been done in the name of Christ. But did you know that it was Christians who founded the first hospitals in the Roman Empire? Built hospitals throughout Europe in the Middle Ages? Founded the Red Cross in Switzerland and helped bring it to America? Have you ever heard of Florence Nightingale? She ministered in the name of Jesus Christ and helped revolutionize health care education."

3. Colleges and universities. It's common knowledge that almost all of America's colleges and universities founded prior to the nineteenth century were church-based.[3] Though many have lost their Christian moorings, the Christian identity of their founders is historically well-established. Here are some quick facts on three prominent institutions in America that can serve as illustrations of Christianity's positive contributions to education.[4]

- Harvard University
  Founded in 1636 by Puritan Christians
  Oldest university in America
  Motto: *Veritas* (Truth)

- Yale University
  Founded in 1701 by Congregationalist Christians
  Known as "The Mother of Colleges" due to its graduates having founded or presided over at least forty other colleges.[5]
  Motto: Light and Truth

- Princeton University
  Founded in 1746 by Presbyterian Christians
  Motto: Under the Protection of God She Flourishes

In conversation with a skeptic who's criticizing Christianity for its failures, you can say, "Every worldview and institution has its faults, including Christianity. I acknowledge that. Yet Christians have made major contributions to society, especially in the field of education. Did you know that almost all of the oldest colleges and universities in the country were founded by Christians? That includes Harvard, Yale and Princeton. It's because Christians believed in education."

Again, to describe redemptive uses of the hammer to skeptical friends, you can talk about Habitat for Humanity, health care and education—all major contributions to society (as a mnemonic device, you could memorize the phrase "Habitat, health care, Harvard"). And don't forget about local efforts of Christians serving in your community. I love telling stories about my own church providing free counseling to hurting families and food and clothing to the needy.

As your conversation with a skeptic progresses through these redemptive illustrations, try to draw the dialogue to this point: If I acknowledge Christianity's faults, are you willing to acknowledge its benefits to society?

Now you have something positive to build on. And with a little research you could learn how Christianity has elevated the status of women throughout the centuries (contrary to popular belief), fought hardest against slavery (consider the work of abolitionist William Wilberforce), and contributed more time and money to nonprofit service than any other demographic of society.[6]

Parallels to the hammer. In addition to discussing imposters and redemptive usage, you can also explore a third avenue of fruitful conversation sparked by the hammer image: Go on the offensive by using analogies with absurd conclusions. Thus to the person who says, "Religion has been the cause of every war," with the implication that Christianity is therefore false or is not worthy of consideration for one's life, I reply with one or more of the following:

- Geography has also caused a lot of wars. Neighboring countries can't agree on boundaries, so they fight to the death.

- Economics has played a major role in starting wars as nations dispute over monetary policies and practices.

- Politics has been one of the most prolific international conflict starters. Who would be foolish enough to deny this?

- Science has contributed massively to human destruction through the creation and proliferation of weapons technology.

So should we stop studying geography and economics because they are inherently evil? Should we judge all political institutions—including your favorite party—as guilty merely because politics has been a constant catalyst of war? Or what about science, perhaps the most revered discipline in the entire academy? Shall we abandon it too due to its misapplication?

As Jeffrey Burton Russell points out, "Almost everyone is a hypocrite because almost everybody fails to live up to their own standards. The only people free of hypocrisy are those who have no standards."[7] Thus we find hypocrisy alive and well in every discipline, worldview and ideology. Christians have no special monopoly on such behavior.

And to the person who makes the strange connection between misuse of religion and religion therefore being false, I say, "Are geography, economics, politics and science therefore false? Should I not believe anything I learn in college or grad school about these fields merely because they've been turned at times to harm?" Hopefully, by way of these analogies, your dialogue partners will be able to see the absurdity of their conclusions about religion that arise from the charge of hypocrisy.

One evening at Michigan State University I gave my hypocrisy presentation to an audience that included several atheist students. For their benefit and that of Christian students struggling to respond well to their non-Christian friends, I broke out a well-known hammer illustration that runs parallel to the indictment of Christianity—the indictment of Joseph Stalin.

Historians aren't sure exactly how many human beings were slaughtered, starved to death or sent to the labor camps by the Soviet dictator during his murderous reign. Tens of millions would be no exaggeration.

Stalin, of course, was an atheist.

I have several questions for my atheist friends and acquaintances. One is whether Stalin's horrific record of harm invalidates atheism as a lifestyle. Can atheists be good if Stalin was so bad? Of course they can. They do it all the time. Prison populations in the United States, for example, show low ratios of atheists, while elite institutions of advanced education show high ratios.

A second question is whether atheism is false because of Stalin. In other words, do Stalin's genocidal crimes actually show that God exists? This gets back to the weird connection between hypocrisy and truth mentioned above. Atheists only laugh at me when I suggest that their worldview might be false (and thus theism or something similar true) due to the malpractice of certain figures such as Stalin.

And laugh they should, since I make the suggestion in irony.

In essence, what atheists are saying back to me when I make the analogy to Stalin is, "Rick, don't blame the hammer. Just because some idiot of the twentieth century abused a philosophy of life doesn't mean that particular philosophy is intrinsically bad or false."

Yes, good point!

I could press the hypocrisy question further by moving on from Stalin to Lenin, Hitler, Mao Zedong and Pol Pot, atheists who "starved and murdered more people in the twentieth century than all the combined religious regimes of the world during the previous nineteen centuries. This is not an exaggeration. By the modest estimates of a BBC 'war audit' in 2004, atheist rulers killed as many as 110 million [people]."[8]

Atheists often respond by denying that these men acted because of their atheism. That is, they didn't commit genocide "in the name of atheism." Such a denial would be of little comfort to the surviving relatives of 110 million slaughtered. Additionally, the atrocities these men committed demonstrate what sinful human beings are capable of when they're not accountable to a higher authority— God. So don't be afraid to ask your atheist friends how the horrific statistics might have changed had these dictators been turned somehow to Jesus Christ, who taught his followers to love their enemies (Luke 6:27).

Return with me now to Michigan State. My presentation is over. One of the atheists approaches me with a curious look in his eye, as if he can't quite figure me. "I really liked your talk," he says cautiously. "I've never heard a Christian apologize before. And you made me think pretty hard with that reference to Stalin." Thoughtful atheists at least see the parallels, and this is valuable in conversation.

So when the charge of hypocrisy is made, break out the hammer. A good friend of mine who's not a Christian tends to blame religion for many of society's troubles, so I used the hammer image in a recent conversation. It stopped her in her tracks. She just looked at me and said, "I never thought of it that way before." Quite probably your friends haven't either.

CHAPTER SUMMARY

Here are strategies to use when skeptical friends level charges of hypocrisy against Christianity as a whole:

Acknowledge harm. When critics bring up examples of Christians behaving badly, don't go on the defensive. Acknowledge real harm done and apologize.

Don't blame the hammer. Use the hammer illustration to help critics see that sinful human beings are to blame for misusing Christianity, not Christianity itself.

Reject imposters. Tell critics that we cannot be responsible for damage done by imposters—those who are not true followers of Jesus. A good analogy is the scenario of fake cops victimizing you in your home. It would be unreasonable to blame the real cops for this crime.

Use redemptive illustrations. Remember the three H's: Habitat, health care, Harvard. These are examples of positive contributions Christianity has made to society, which is important when critics put the faith in a negative light.

Point out parallels. These would include other endeavors misused by sinful human beings to cause injury and death, such as economics, politics and science. Additionally, 110 million people slaughtered by twentieth-century dictators should count decisively against the exclusive blame placed on religion for the world's ills, demonstrating that no ideology is immune to the charge of hypocrisy—certainly not atheism.

SUGGESTED RESOURCES

Alvin J. Schmidt, *How Christianity Changed the World* (Grand Rapids, MI: Zondervan, 2009).

Jeffrey Burton Russell, *Exposing Myths About Christianity: A Guide to Answering 145 Viral Lies and Legends* (Downers Grove, IL: IVP Books, 2012).

9

RELIGIONS ARE LIKE BOOKS

And Other Images for
Discussing Religious Pluralism

IT WAS A SOFT AUTUMN AFTERNOON when I visited one of the top
academic schools in America—the University of Chicago—and
toured its enchanted grounds with my friend Lauren. As we wan-
dered the campus I was spellbound by the classic gothic majesty
of the buildings, some of them more than a hundred years old,
others more modern but created in the original style.

At an appointed time, Lauren guided me into the Reynolds Club
student center, a cathedral-like edifice that houses, among other
things, a coffee shop on the second floor called Hallowed Grounds.
There she introduced me to a first-year student named Ann and left.

An international student and daughter of professionals, Ann had
been well-educated in her home country. She'd been reading Nietzsche.
I found her to be a mix of Renaissance and postmodernity, a truly global
citizen, tolerant of many viewpoints, pluralistic to the core. At my request, she sketched out her religious philosophy—impressively so, with
the articulation of a thirty-year-old grad student, though she was but in
her late teens. Then she said quite simply, "What do you think?"

I didn't answer at first; I was too busy processing the multiple
sensations of this remarkable setting, of the brilliant young inter-
nationalist across the table, and . . . damnable self-doubt. I was a
little off my equilibrium.

But in God conversations there's usually no hurry. You can take the time you need to say the right thing, and even if it isn't the right thing, better to pause than to jump into the fray rashly.

Finally I spoke. I asked Ann how she handled contradictions between religions, then I named a few. She replied that contradictions don't really matter, because it's not exactly the "method" that counts in finding God, just that you find him.

I replied that religions are like books. Walk into the religion section of a bookstore or library and you'll notice that the covers are similar in appearance. They all say something about finding God or transcendence or mystical secrets or Brahman and so on, and to the novice these words sound roughly equivalent and interchangeable. But when you actually open the books and read their contents, you find that the accounts they give of reality are radically divergent. Some tell you that God is one, others that God is many. Some have no God at all. One says desire is the basic human problem, another says disobedience, another sin. Solutions to the human problem vary. The account of the origin of the universe is quite different in Judaism than, say, Buddhism. In fact, it's jolting to even compare the two, as if their doctrines come to us from different worlds, which maybe they do. And what about the concept of time: Is it linear? Cyclical? Illusory? Depends which book you read. As Stephen Prothero has noted, "If practitioners of the world's religions are all mountain climbers, then they are on very different mountains, climbing very different peaks."[1]

On a piece of scratch paper I drew the following diagram:

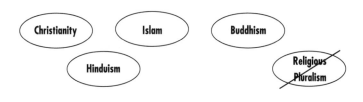

Figure 2.

Religious pluralism is the idea that all religions are valid in their own way. I noted that if we take seriously the contradictions between religions, then the one single view in the entire diagram that cannot be true is that they're all true. In other words, religious pluralism cannot be true.

Now it was Ann's turn to pause. She looked at the diagram in silence. I suppose one could say that the answers to the cosmos (and beyond) were contained in that rough little sketch. Somewhere. I broke in as gently as I could: "As you can see, everything depends on whether contradictions between the religions matter. If they matter, religious pluralism is in trouble. And, of course,

Religions Are All the Same?
The Buildings and Lakes Analogies

Let's say we decide not to take the contradictions between religions seriously. Or we decide to water down all religions to a collection of great moral platitudes, such as love for God and neighbor. Either way, religious pluralism is back in play. It's sort of like saying that all buildings in a city look roughly the same from a 30,000-foot flyover. Then we mistakenly conclude that they really are all the same and we ignore the fact that one is an office building, another a factory, another a restaurant. One building is focused on software development, its neighbor down the street on auto repair. Sure, if you ignore the particularities— the distinctives—of the individual businesses, they're all "pretty much the same." But have you really said anything meaningful? I suppose bodies of water, too, look the same on the surface, but of course they differ sharply when you take the time to dive into their depths for a firsthand look. Lake Johanna, a small recreational lake near my house, versus Lake Superior? Not even close, except for some generalities they have in common: water, plants and fish.

contradictions do matter. They always matter."

The logic of the diagram is tough to argue with. Even so, I was a bit startled when Ann made her move, concluding (with me) that no, all the views couldn't be true—except in the most general and trivial way, like book covers are similar. Suddenly finding herself in a new position, she looked up with a smile: "That makes me a consumer."

I liked that. "Consumer" is the right word. She was a "shopper of religions" in the mall of great spiritual traditions. If only she knew which one to buy. Ann was an economics major, very practical in her thinking, so she was all about achieving maximum benefit for her efforts and investments. Which religion should she pick? Which would pay off most?

She asked if I would serve as her guide. "Love to," I replied. "But you have to know, I'm not exactly an unbiased adviser. I'm already inside one of the religions." Then I told her that I could provide some excellent reasons to believe in Jesus. She said okay, so I did. Then things got interesting. She replied, astutely, "What if you're wrong? What if Christianity isn't the right choice? Like, what if it's not even true?"

"Then I've held to something false most of my life and promoted it to others."

"I can't believe you just said that! I've never heard a Christian say that before. Are you saying it's possible that you're wrong?"

"Sure."

Let's hit the pause button for a second. Obviously I don't think Christianity is false. If that's what I thought, I wouldn't be a Christian. But is it theoretically possible that Rick Mattson, prone to sin and errors in judgment, has chosen the wrong option? Of course.

Back to our story. Ann smiled broadly and looked at the diagram while I leaned forward to avoid the back end of a cue stick that was oscillating near my head. I thought it odd that the smartest students in America (or close to it) played pool.

"Rick, would other Christians say what you just said? Like the Pope?"

"Hard to speak for the Pope, Ann. But I'm guessing if he were sitting in the chair right there and talking only to the two of us, and not to thousands where his meaning could be misconstrued, he'd agree with me."

"Okay," she said, nodding. "Religious pluralism is the one option that can't be true. I understand that now. Wow, I think I've really gotten somewhere today. I never expected this."

Gosh, me neither.

So what just happened? This conversation is a good example of the need to take things one step at a time. Don't get ahead of yourself. Ann went from pluralist to nonpluralist, not from pluralist to Christian. A main purpose of apologetics is to clear space for belief. In this case, the barrier was pluralism. We needed to deal with that first. I'm always looking for the first sticking point in the framework of unbelief in another person. It's good to honor the particulars of their skepticism as an important part of who they are.

I like to use the "religions are like books" analogy whenever anyone thinks all religions are roughly the same. It helps counter the popular notion that religions are different on the surface but the same underneath. In fact, it's more correct to say that religions are similar on the surface (like book covers) and different underneath (like the contents of the books).[2] When Ann saw that, it made a huge difference.

IS PLURALISM EGALITARIAN? INCLUSIVE? THE KNOW-IT-ALL (PART 1)

There's an interactive talk I've given many times on college campuses called "The Challenge of Other Religions." The talk centers around a philosopher who is arguably the world's foremost religious pluralist: John Hick. Usually no one has heard of him. Too bad for them. He's a great read. After a little bio sketch of Dr. Hick, including his upbringing in the Christian faith and his subsequent rejection of the historic doctrine of the incarnation, I diagram his model of religious pluralism on a whiteboard. It's similar to the diagram I drew for Ann, as you can see below.

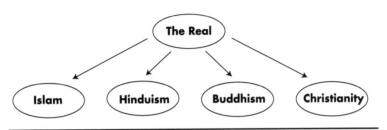

Figure 3.

In Hick's model, "The Real" at the top of the diagram represents God or transcendent reality. The Real reveals itself to the world's major religions, and each responds from within its own cultural context. These varied contexts are what account for the differences (even contradictions) between religions.

Hick's model sounds appealing at first: God, or the Real, actually exists. Check. The Real discloses itself to all the big players—Islam, Hinduism, Buddhism, Judaism, Christianity. Check. Each religion interprets the Real through the lens of its own unique culture. Check. Logical tensions between the traditions reflect the diversity of cultures in which they were founded and developed. In short, the Real plus culture equals religious pluralism. All views are valid; none is superior to the others; no one has a monopoly on the truth . . . everybody wins. It all makes sense.

Yes, it makes sense until you start asking some probing questions. Invariably during the presentation some brave soul will wrinkle her face, raise her hand and begin her first sentence with the word "but." "But what about other religions not mentioned? What about suicide cults—do they also receive divine revelation? Why or why not?" Other students chime in: "Where does Hick himself fit into the diagram? Doesn't all this imply that one view really is superior to the others—Hick's?"

Now I am here to tell you that Hick is brilliant and he's aware of these critiques, and in my presentation I don't make it easy on students who are skeptical of his model. I defend him for a while, as best I can, but as the hour winds down I side with the critics and give the analogy of the know-it-all.

Let's say a Muslim friend—we'll call him Khalid—and I are having a respectful but pointed dialogue on the topic of salvation. He says to me, "Rick, unless you confess the *shahada*—that God is one and Muhammad is his prophet—and submit your will to Allah, you will die in your sins." Wow, there's honesty for you, and I love it. I need more friends like that. So I return the favor: "Khalid, unless you repent and believe in Jesus as your Lord and Savior, you will die in your sins."

Khalid and I know we have a contradiction on our hands. He's saying that Christian salvation is false and Islamic salvation is true. I'm saying just the opposite. Thus, our views are mutually exclusive.

But then a third-party interloper comes along and begins to tell us our business. He tells us that our two ways of salvation represent parallel paths to the top of the same mountain. We don't actually need to resolve our differences but rather we should accept the essential validity of each other's perspectives.

Khalid and I look at each other, then we tell the interloper (Hick) to put a muzzle on it. How does he know our stuff better than we do? Is he going to water down our traditions so they blend together into some kind of grayish-brown mush? Or maybe he thinks our disagreement about salvation is merely a function of cultural variation? We disagree. Only a know-it-all would pretend to understand our own traditions better than we do. Ironically, the original appeal of Hick's proposal—that it's inclusive and egalitarian—is defeated by the arrogance of the know-it-all who looks down from his perch and tells everyone how things really are. We say back to him, "You may be one of us, but you're not above us." That is, pluralism may exist alongside us as one of the contenders, but it has no special privilege to tell everyone else they've got it wrong.

THE BLIND MEN AND THE ELEPHANT: THE KNOW-IT-ALL (PART 2)

I love the parable of the blind men and the elephant because it illustrates the power of illustrations. In the parable, several blind men seek for an understanding of the true nature of an elephant, which represents God. One man grabs the tail and declares that the elephant is like a rope. Another gets hold of the trunk and says that, no, the elephant is more like a large tree branch. The story continues with the great creature's legs (pillars), tusks (pipes) and ears (giant fans) being misunderstood by the other men as the true nature of the elephant.

For the pluralist, the parable illustrates the idea that each religion thinks it possesses the whole truth, when in fact each has only a piece of the puzzle. A humble recognition of this fact from all of the religions would promote interfaith dialogue and lead to a more comprehensive understanding of God for everyone.

The status of this parable in higher education is nothing short of iconic. Professors and students in sociology, anthropology and religion classes can recite it on cue against the exclusive claims of any religion, most notably Christianity. Ironically, the story is often told with the same level of confidence possessed by the blind men whose chief fault is overconfidence.

As for myself, a Christian apologist in the academy, I have no problem with the concept of learning helpful truths from other religions. In fact, at Macalester College in Minnesota, my home base, I actively seek perspectives different from my own and I treasure friendships with those of neighboring faiths.

But again, something's wrong with this picture. Why think the men in the parable (who represent leaders of various faith traditions) are blind? How would the storyteller know this? Apparently the storyteller knows a lot more about the elephant than any of the blind men. In other words, the pluralist who is telling the story claims to have insights into the nature of God (or gods, or the Real) that none of the faith traditions possess. That's a gigantic truth claim. Only a special, enlightened individual would make such a claim. Or a know-it-all.

THE DOCTOR

Biblical Christianity makes certain truth claims that are exclusive. The main one is that the only true path to salvation is through Jesus Christ. Most Christians who take the Bible as the Word of God agree with this claim, and when they verbalize it publicly they're accused of being arrogant and intolerant. I heard it again on talk radio the other day (on a sports program, no less): "Just practice your own religion and leave it at that. Why do you have to insist that everyone else is wrong?"

The thing is, I'm not the one making the exclusive claim about salvation—Jesus is. He is the one who said, "I am the way and the truth and the life. No one comes to the Father except through me" (John 14:6). I'm simply trusting his authority to know these things. It's like going to my excellent family physician, Dr. Lehman. If he tells me my cholesterol is too high and that I need to cut down on sweets and fatty foods, I believe him. He's an expert on the matter. Sure, there are plenty of other voices I could listen to about my health, including celebrities, infomercials and tabloid articles. To the extent that these voices disagree with Dr. Lehman, they're most likely wrong. My physician has made the "exclusive" claim that his patient, me, has a certain malady that requires a certain treatment. I'm just the amateur who believes him.

This analogy can work with any authority figure you can think of: pilot, air traffic controller, professor, lawyer, scientist, astronaut, boat captain and so on. I prefer the doctor image because it's so universally revered—and because I can remember it easily: Jesus, of course, is known as the Great Physician.

I suppose a skeptic could push back on the analogy by pointing out that sometimes doctors are wrong and that at the very least one should get a second opinion. That's fine. The point is that somewhere in the process I, the amateur, trust in some authority who makes an exclusive truth claim about my condition. And to the extent that I make real life choices with my time and money to pursue the prescribed treatment, I've trusted in that authority. Indeed, it would seem foolish to validate the diagnostics of all the other conflicting voices—celebrities, infomercials, tabloids—as being equally "truthful."

A second objection is that it's not obvious Jesus would be the one to turn to as the expert on salvation. Why not Muhammad, the Buddha, Krishna or others? Actually, it's not uncommon for Christian thinkers to value insights from traditions other than Christianity. Noted pastor Timothy Keller, for instance, reminds us that all human beings are made in the image of God, that non-believers are therefore capable of living exemplary lives and that Christianity provides a "firm basis for respecting people of other faiths."[3] An example from Scripture is the Roman centurion Cornelius, who is described as "devout and God-fearing" and whose prayers and gifts to the poor are rewarded by God with a personal audience with the apostle Peter.

The story doesn't stop there, however. The centurion's prayers and good works do not in themselves merit salvation, but rather an invitation from Peter to believe in Christ—which Cornelius and his family accept (see Acts 10). This should reinforce to us the point that whatever the positive contributions of other religious traditions to the ethical framework of society, the road to salvation must always go through Jesus. If he really is the unique, revealed Son of God made flesh, then he stands as the expert on salvation, and it's imperative that we pay close attention to his teaching.

Bottom line on Christian exclusivity: Deflect the charge of arrogance and exclusivity onto Jesus, your true doctor. He can take the heat.

CHAPTER SUMMARY

It should be noted that many people who are religious pluralists are *inside* one of the faith camps. That is, they believe in one of the Christian denominations or other religious traditions. That's a bit different than dealing with hardened skeptics. My advice to you, born of decades of experience in this arena, is to be gentle. Choose your words carefully. Make a friend, form a partnership, work together, walk humbly. Adopt a true learning posture. If you offer deference to the other person, he or she will usually give it in return. That doesn't mean you give up your distinctive Christian beliefs. On the contrary, who would respect such wishy-washiness? Learn the art of respectful disagreement.

Pluralistic Objection	Image to Use
Religions are all the same.	Religions are like books: If you go to the religion section of a bookstore, the covers of the books are broadly similar. But when you open the books and read the contents, they tell radically different stories about reality.
	So are buildings viewed from 30,000 feet. But when you examine the buildings up close, you find that the businesses they house are quite distinct from each other.
	So are bodies of water, but only in a general and trivial sense: When you compare a small local lake with, say, Lake Superior or an ocean, about the only things they have in common are water, plants and fish (though not even the same plants and fish).
Pluralism is true because it's egalitarian and inclusive.	The know-it-all (part 1): The pluralist claims to know more about all the religions (and God) than the believers in those religions. Thus, while coming to us in the guise of being egalitarian and inclusive, the pluralist is actually quite arrogant to tell us our business. He comes off as a know-it-all.
The challenge of the blind men and the elephant.	The know-it-all (part 2): The storyteller seems to know more about the elephant (God) than anyone else. Another example of a know-it-all.

Pluralistic Objection	Image to Use
Christians are exclusive and arrogant.	The doctor: When my doctor makes an "exclusive" diagnosis and prescribes a treatment, I believe him. That doesn't make me arrogant. In the same way, when Jesus claims to be the only path to salvation, my belief in him doesn't make me arrogant. I'm just the amateur exercising faith in the expert.

SUGGESTED RESOURCES

Stephen Prothero, *God Is Not One: The Eight Rival Religions That Run the World—and Why Their Differences Matter* (New York: HarperCollins, 2010).

Timothy Keller, *The Reason for God* (New York: Dutton, 2008), chap. 1.

Douglas Groothuis, *Christian Apologetics: A Comprehensive Case for Biblical Faith* (Downers Grove, IL: IVP Academic, 2011), chap. 23.

CAN THOSE WHO'VE NEVER HEARD OF JESUS BE SAVED?

The Homeless Person Analogy

A FEW MONTHS AGO I was fueling my Ford Explorer at a gas station in my neighborhood when a disheveled woman who seemed very sad approached me. She needed a ride to her sister's apartment a mile away. Her weight posed a serious challenge to entering the passenger side of my SUV, but somehow she mounted the step and squeezed in. We made small talk for five minutes during the ride over to her sister's place. It was a high-rise apartment. She pulled out a phone and called her sister. No answer. She said she'd wait it out in the lobby of the high-rise until her sister showed and thanked me for the lift. Before exiting the SUV she made a certain request of me that, no doubt, she'd made many times before, probably successfully.

I left the scene twenty dollars lighter in the wallet, choosing not to call her bluff but just thinking to myself that maybe this was God shedding light from an unlikely source into a part of my life that can be quite dark. You see, I'm actually pretty good at not seeing large, destitute women loitering in my pathway along Snelling Avenue—a busy thoroughfare in my town.

THE OBJECTION

It seems to me that the ability to see God is roughly analogous to seeing a homeless person. Both are hidden in plain sight—there for the taking but often missed. Later in the chapter I'll show how this analogy can help us reply to critics who protest God's (supposed) condemnation of those who've never heard of Christ. Here's a version of the critic's objection: Billions of people live their lives out of range of the gospel message—an accident of birth that's no fault of their own. Surely they cannot be condemned for their lack of knowledge or faith by the Christian God, who is supposedly loving and just. Essentially, this objection is about lack of opportunity.

THE REPLY

As a Christian, I begin my response with these two assertions: (1) I don't know who is and who is not saved, because that's God's business. (2) No one is saved outside of the work of Christ. In conversation, these starting points put me on solid apologetic footing because they rightly take me out of the business of judgmentalism (I don't judge who's saved), plus I'm simply being honest about the exclusive claim that Jesus makes to be the Savior of the world.

To the religious pluralist, then, who believes other religions also provide valid and sufficient means of reaching the religious goal—such as heaven or nirvana or oneness with the universe or ultimate peace—I point out that the world's religions cannot all be deeply true because they contradict each other, as we just discussed in chapter nine. Furthermore, if it can be established that Jesus was God in the flesh and rose from the dead, then his words "I am the way and the truth and the life. No one comes to the Father except through me" (John 14:6) should be taken as true, and the pluralist should consider revising his views accordingly.

Similarly, to the universalist who says that God saves everyone, no matter their beliefs, I point to the many "judgment passages" in the New Testament that seem to indicate otherwise, such as Matthew 5:22, 29-30. It's difficult to maintain a universalist position if one truly believes in the teachings of the New Testament.

Perhaps a critic doesn't believe in Jesus at all, however, so you may be wondering why I'm referencing Jesus in my reply. In the long run, an apologetic for Christ being the Son of God may have to be covered (see chapter five). But remember the explicit objection at the moment is not about God's existence or the identity of Jesus, but whether in biblical Christianity there is condemnation for those who've never heard the gospel. That's the specific issue of our focus.

GOD'S ACTIONS

It's important to note in conversation that God is the one who takes initiative to reveal himself to people. Certainly he does not leave us on our own to figure things out, as if to say, "Find me if you can. You'll get no help from me." On the contrary, he has done much to reveal himself and empower our faith, as follows:

1. *Providing clues.* I often point out to critics that God leaves clues of his presence, even to those who've never learned about Christ. Clues, mind you, not proof. Proof would coerce belief. Theologian Greg Boyd observes, "[God] is present enough so that those who want to experience Him can experience Him, but absent enough so that those who don't want to experience Him aren't forced to. . . . [God's] love requires both evidence and hiddenness."[1] In other words, God is a respecter of persons; he doesn't overwhelm our ability to say no, doesn't force himself on us, but rather invites us into a relationship by placing indicators— clues of his love and grace—in our path. One might say he "woos" rather than "overrules."

What are these clues? They're found in what theologians call "general revelation," defined as nature and conscience.[2] Nature, of course, refers to the world around us. The psalmist puts it best:

The heavens declare the glory of God;
    the skies proclaim the work of his hands.
Day after day they pour forth speech. (Psalm 19:1-2)

Thus nature serves as a platform for showcasing God's presence and glory. Conscience refers to the law of God written on the human heart. Having been created by God, we possess a deep, built-in sense of morality, even if we often ignore this intuition (see Romans 2:14-15).

Here's the point about general revelation: it's available to everyone. Everyone can see the glory of God in nature and discern the law of God in conscience. General revelation is *universal* revelation, as Paul indicates in Romans 1:20: "For since the creation of the world God's invisible qualities—his eternal power and divine nature—have been clearly seen, being understood from what has been made, so that people are without excuse." Note the phrase "clearly seen" in that verse. It speaks of the accessibility of God's revelation to everyone.

Everyone who's looking, that is.

And this raises the question of why someone might be looking for God in the first place. If humans suffer from a spiritual sickness called sin, if their natural bent is to live for themselves—or, on their best days, live for others—what would cause them to even care about God? How could the unholy turn itself to the holy? Isn't it in the very nature of sin to turn away from God, not toward him?

Perhaps there is a way. Perhaps God himself initiates the possibility of human transformation without coercing belief. Maybe God has a special grace designed just for this purpose.

2. Providing grace: the prison key image. Kreeft and Tacelli note that God "plants grace" in the human heart so that those who seek him possess abilities beyond their own ability to find the truth.[3] Sometimes this is called "prevenient grace"—that is, "preceding" grace, or grace that "goes ahead" and jump-starts the process of faith.[4] Think of this image: human beings are imprisoned in their own fallen nature and are unable and unwilling to seek after God. So God uses the "prison key" of grace to release them to respond to him. He lets them out of the slammer into the light of day where they can see more clearly.

Ephesians 2:8 lays it out for us: "For it is by grace you have been saved, through faith—and this is not from yourselves." Far from waiting for us to seek him, God actively seeks us, and perhaps we respond in faith. This should be good to news to anyone who thinks it's entirely up to busy, distracted, sinful, preoccupied, messy human beings to discover God by their own limited powers.

3. *Providing signs.* Going along with this grace is a factor I call "divine serendipity." This refers to circumstantial evidence of God's hand operating in a person's life—signs, one might say. Signs need not be spectacular, though sometimes they are. And of course they are open to interpretation from a non-Christian standpoint as mere coincidence.

A few years ago I was part of an evangelism project in Aspen, Colorado. Two members of our team, Jennifer and Rich, approached a father and his young boy sitting quietly on a park bench. Turns out the man had custody of his son for the weekend and they were resting after a vigorous hike. Sitting at their feet, Jennifer looked up and asked the man what he thought of God.

"Interesting that you should ask," the man replied. "On the way over the mountain this morning, my son asked me the same question. I said I'd give him an answer when we returned to this side."

In my view it was God who stirred the heart of a young boy to ask his father such a profound question in the first place. And perhaps during the trek over the mountain and back, father and son were awed by the beauty and glory of nature. And perhaps their "chance" encounter with our team was God's way of providing a hurting father with a sign of divine compassion and a gentle summons to faith.

So far we've looked at three responses to the charge that God condemns those who, through no fault of their own, live out of range of the gospel message: clues to his existence, grace like a prison key, and signs of his hand at work. Certain pieces of the puzzle are still missing, however. Specifically, what does it take from a human perspective to find God? We've looked briefly at God's actions, but what about ours? To the issue at hand, what steps are required of people who've never heard the gospel message? Can their faith response to "general revelation" lead to salvation—or will they be condemned?

THE HOMELESS PERSON ANALOGY

Human responsibility in the faith equation is, I believe, analogous to seeing a homeless person on a street corner. Talk about hidden in plain sight! Even after using this analogy in many conversations (and writing about it), I have a hard time seeing these folks. Is it because they're invisible? Not at all. In fact, their goal is high visibility. They don't hold up "Hungry, please help" signs in dark alleys and under bridges. Rather, they take their message to the masses at prominent intersections.

As I pull up to them in my vehicle, a recording plays in my head, something like this: "I'm busy and in a hurry. . . . I already give my tithe to God's work elsewhere. . . . If I give cash to the destitute they'll just blow it on cigarettes and booze. . . . What good would a donation do anyway? Handouts don't get to the root of the problem. This guy will just be hungry tomorrow again. . . . He should try getting a job. . . . Maybe I should give away nonperishable food items. . . . Nah, it's a hassle. . . . This isn't my deal. . . . I wonder what's for supper."

After the fiftieth or hundredth instance of this routine, I no longer see the poor, no longer go through my list of excuses and denials, though they remain in my subconscious. It's the same with seeing God. People are preoccupied with their own lives to the point where God's "eternal power and divine nature" (Romans 1:20) are not clearly seen, though he is "not far from any one of us" (Acts 17:27). Yes, God is there for the seeing, hidden in plain view, but it takes spiritual insight to actually notice him—what Jesus calls "eyes to see." And this is tied to the condition of one's heart. The crucial question becomes whether a person actually wants to find God. It's a matter of the will. Many do not care for such a search. But if they truly seek him—with the help of God's grace— they will be rewarded. As Jesus teaches, "Seek and you will find; knock and the door will be opened to you. . . . The one who seeks finds" (Matthew 7:7-8).

So to answer the objection that a loving God wouldn't condemn those who haven't heard the gospel, I appeal to the homeless man analogy. Anyone can find God if they humble themselves and seek the truth. Kreeft and Tacelli summarize the process:

1. *Seek.* Going after the truth is actually going after God, be- cause God is the truth. Such truth seeking is motivated by the will, which indicates the presence of divine grace in the seeking soul.

2. *Repent.* Repentance results when a person recognizes his or her failure to measure up to the law of God within and the excellence of nature without, and that person feels remorse. Isaiah brings together seeking and repentance as follows:

Seek the LORD while he may be found;
   call on him while he is near.
Let the wicked forsake their ways [repentance]
   and the unrighteous their thoughts.
Let them turn to the LORD, and he will have mercy on them.
   (Isaiah 55:6-7)

3. *Respond in faith.* The person responds by believing in the Creator and moral law.[5]

Thoughtful Christians and some theologically informed non-Christians may wonder at this point whether faith in a generalized notion of God is actually enough. Is faith in a vague creator figure or, say, in the "higher power" of Alcoholics Anonymous acceptable to God? Will this faith save? It's a thorny question and I mention it not to add to the long-standing debate on the issue, but because it comes up in conversation with critics.

SAVING FAITH?

A word about Christian exclusivity is in order before we take on the question of whether faith in God through general revelation is sufficient for salvation. Since I don't hold to the pluralist position—that other religions save—or the universalist position—that all are saved—I am an exclusivist. As a general rule in Western culture, exclusivity is denounced, inclusivity embraced. Most everyone wants to be seen as "inclusive" these days, and rightly so when it comes to issues such as ethnic diversity, educational and job opportunities and human rights.

But in matters of religion, everyone is exclusive at some level. For example, the pluralist who believes that many or all religions save must at some point reject (exclude) my form of Christianity, which says that only Jesus saves. In other words, if religious pluralism is true, Christianity as actually practiced by billions of Christians like myself is false. That's a very exclusive claim. Ironically, it comes in the guise of pluralism, which has a reputation for being open and inclusive.

So I make no apology for being an exclusivist. We all are. But that doesn't mean I wish ill for any person on the salvation question at hand. Additionally, as discussed in chapter nine, I'm not the one making exclusive claims for Christianity, Jesus is. He is the one who claimed to be the only path to God. He is the expert authority on these matters, which he established through his teachings and resurrection, and I am just the amateur who believes him.

So from this exclusivist standpoint, does faith in God based on general revelation—without specific knowledge of Jesus—save? I don't know. But I do know these two things: God is loving and just and his will is that none should perish (2 Peter 3:9). Second, God seems to care about how people respond to the light they've received, in whatever amount.

In the famous parable of the talents, for instance, the servants who invest the resources they've been given by their master are rewarded with more, while the servant who buries his share in the ground is judged harshly (Matthew 25:14-30). It's a stewardship issue. "For whoever has will be given more, and they will have an abundance. Whoever does not have, even what they have will be taken from them" (Matthew 25:29).

I find this principle of stewarding resources in the gospels both hopeful and sobering. It gives me hope that those who've never heard of Christ can well steward their given share of revelation and receive the gift of salvation. But it also reminds me that those who do nothing with their share of revelation—who fail to see God hidden in plain view (the homeless man image)—will be judged for their sin.

Theologian David Clark is cautiously optimistic about the fate of those who have lived their lives out of range of the gospel message but are seekers of God.

> [God's] deep divine passion is to rescue all people. If we start with what we know, we can gain confidence. Somehow—it's speculation to say exactly how—God is at work to draw all people to himself. . . . The clear part is that God has instructed Christians to offer others the opportunity to receive the gift of salvation. The less clear part is what God is doing behind the scenes. If God's character and intentions are as the Bible says [God's justice is intensely opposed to evil; God's grace is expressed in a passionate love for people], I surmise God is doing far more than we know.[6]

Clark is trying here to address both the known and the unknown. We know and understand the calling and obligation for Christians to share the gospel message with the whole world. This is non-negotiable. And we know the character of God as both just and loving. What's unknown is what other means God may be using to reach out to his fallen creatures. Clark concludes that God "draws all repentant people to himself. . . . I believe God will give the chance to all. We don't know how this works."[7]

A REAL PERSON

It's easy in some respects to speak of salvation as an abstract concept. But here's a real-life example. "Grandmother," as she was known by many, was a woman living in a country of southeast Asia that was culturally Buddhist. She was strong and healthy until the final two months of her life and had survived three of her four children. Missionaries prayed for her salvation—and for those she would influence, since as the matriarch of the family she had the power to release other relatives to seek after God. During those last two months of physical suffering, Grandmother saw several visions of Jesus—one with four holy men in white robes, another where the Lord came and sat at the head of her bed in silence, bringing comfort and healing.

Her pain vanished for several weeks but finally returned, intensely so. The missionaries asked God to relieve her suffering and take her if it was her time to go. She died on an Easter Sunday at the age of 102. A relative said afterward, "Although Grandmother had never read books about God or been to church, she knew Jesus when she saw him and she recognized him as one who was holy, powerful and special beyond others."

This real-life story reminds me of the variables and complexities of the human condition as it relates to God and salvation. Grandmother had lived a long life, a good life, yet had missed God for an entire century. The prayers of missionaries, the unseen "prevenient grace" in her life that unlocked her spiritual sight, the visions of Jesus (again, the homeless man analogy applies), the pain that perhaps forced her to look to God for relief . . . Who knows, really, what was happening in the spiritual realm? We are wise to exercise humility when it comes to knowing exactly how this whole process works. Ours is a smallish, confined perspective, while God's is complete and exhaustive.

CHAPTER SUMMARY

The main objection from a critic is that a loving, good God would not condemn the billions of people who've never had the chance to hear the gospel message. Essentially, this is the "lack of opportunity" objection.

First reply. God initiates with us with clues, grace and signs.

Second reply. We have a responsibility to respond to God's initiative by noticing and believing in him. He is hidden in plain sight, just like a homeless man or woman.

Third reply. God is loving and just and desires all to be saved. He works in ways we do not know or understand to draw all people to himself. Thus it's likely that everyone at least has the opportunity for salvation.

SUGGESTED RESOURCES

J. P. Moreland and William Lane Craig, *Philosophical Foundations for a Christian Worldview* (Downers Grove, IL: IVP Academic, 2003), chap. 31.

Peter Kreeft and Ronald Tacelli, *Handbook of Christian Apologetics* (Downers Grove, IL: InterVarsity Press, 1994), chap. 13.

David Clark, *To Know and Love God* (Wheaton, IL: Crossway, 2010), chap. 10.

Francis J. Beckwith, William Lane Craig and J. P. Moreland, *To Everyone an Answer* (Downers Grove, IL: IVP Academic, 2004), chap. 17.

11

HELL IS LIKE AN EMPTY PUB

ON MOTHER'S DAY, CIRCA 2001, an elderly woman stepped out of the clubhouse into the bright sunshine at Mississippi Dunes Golf Links, which overlooks the expansive backwaters of the Mississippi River near Cottage Grove, Minnesota. She had just finished a lovely brunch and was headed to the parking lot when she bumped into a golfer. She decided to ask him what he and his friends were doing, playing golf on Mother's Day. "I guess we're orphans," quipped the man.

The name stuck. I joined the Orphans in 2005. The group consists of about a dozen golfers—not exactly the twelve apostles, I can tell you. They welcomed me into their midst at a time when my own group had ditched me for greener pastures at another golf course. The Orphans call me a holy man and a saint, but I deny these titles and tell them that I'm a sinner just like them—a forgiven sinner, thanks be to Jesus, but a sinner nonetheless.

Salty sailors, this lot; the Orphans like to party. Their annual banquet feast is held on a Sunday in early October, and one year due to church commitments I showed up late to the festivities. Four long tables had been set in a square in a private room of the clubhouse, and I was aware of a few smart-aleck greetings as I took a seat next to my pal Donnie, who had a pint or two under his belt already. With a smirky grin he motioned his hand across the room and observed that this whole scene must be quite a shock to my system, having just arrived from church. I replied that Jesus was always hanging out with sinners, and that he'd feel right at home here with the Orphans, as did I.

Jesus was criticized by the religious establishment for lounging around with tax collectors and sinners, and he was called a glutton and a drunkard (Matthew 11:19). Exaggeration, no doubt. Still, before we turn him into an ascetic like John the Baptist, we should remember the story where Jesus infuses 150 gallons of wine into a dying wedding celebration in Cana of Galilee (John 2:1-11). I'd never say Jesus came to earth mainly to party, because people could misconstrue your meaning. But I am saying that he frequented a lot of parties and was comfortable there—and I could sense his presence with me at the Orphans' banquet feast on this Lord's day at Mississippi Dunes.

Sometimes I ask college students where Jesus would spend most of his time were he still here in the flesh: in churches or bars? The conservative ones say "churches" and the progressive ones say "bars," and I say that he'd be in both places quite a lot.

I remember looking around the room fondly at my golfing pals: chowing down on steak and shrimp, polishing off strong drink, maybe telling a joke or two I won't recount, and occasionally mentioning my nickname—as in, "Hey, Rev, pass the rolls." Yeah, they call me the Rev. And despite my having a mostly religious profile, they treat me like one of the gang. Well, mostly. I'm told there's a certain email list that circulates special "information" to the guys that seems to skip my inbox, which is probably just as well.

I just wonder whether I'll see most of them in the afterlife. There's a kind of attitude in secular culture that is summed up by the Satan character in Milton's *Paradise Lost*: "Better to reign in Hell than to serve in heaven." Except these days the devil's words have been slightly reworked into something like this: I'd rather party with my friends in hell than get bored in heaven.

But according to Jesus, this is exactly where a great surprise will take place in the afterlife. Hell, you see, is not a perpetual party. It's more like an empty pub.

It might be more than that. Hell might be worse. Depending on how literally you take biblical images such as a blazing furnace, flesh-eating worms and outer darkness, hell might consist of real torment.[1]

But at the very least, hell is a place of isolation and loneliness. It's reserved for the person who's said no to the God of community and to the Jesus who loves a good party. It's a place that awaits the person who's insisted on living on his own terms, making his own parties, abiding by his own rules.[2] Quite simply, hell is for the person who thinks he's wiser than Jesus.

A PARABLE ABOUT BEN

During Ben's first day in hell he feels a sense of freedom. He's finally rid of God and all his influence and rules and judgments. Forever. On his way to the hell pub, Ben reflects on how the good times will be even sweeter down here. Earthly constraints are gone. No job or family responsibilities to get in the way, no morning hangover to avoid, no conscience to appease, no deity to evade. He can finally let loose.

His mouth waters at the prospect of joining up with his crew again to fulfill an agreement of solidarity made in those last days together on earth. He remembers the final raucous toast of hoisted glasses, fists raised, the boisterous cheers from the bellies of all his mates echoing off the barstools and neon beer signs: "See you in hell! Yeahhhh!" But now, when he bursts through the doorway of the hell bar, his face falls. Something is wrong. It's like a ghost town. Nobody home. He returns the next day and the next, hoping to be reunited with his pals. But they never show, and he drinks alone for weeks and months and years—and more. Ben loses hope as he senses his soul shrinking, slipping away into oblivion.

Melodrama? Perhaps. The point is that if you're in hell, the God who created you to live in relationships and community is gone. God himself is the ultimate model of community, for God is Trinity—three persons in one being.[3] Thus to be made "in his image" is to be made, among other things, for community, for connectivity, for time with others. Even a reserved personality who enjoys time alone (such as myself) needs, at some level, the company of fellow human beings in order to live properly before God. In the New Testament, this togetherness among believers is called the body of Christ (see 1 Corinthians 12:12-27; Romans 12:4-9). It means that each person is called to live and serve in a fellowship of interconnected and interdependent parts that reflect the image of God as Christ's body in the world.

WHAT THE EMPTY PUB IMAGE ACCOMPLISHES

In saying that hell is like an empty pub, I'm doing two things: (1) offering up a description of hell as being at least the absence of God, while leaving room for possible more severe realities (such as conscious torment), as mentioned above, and (2) targeting especially seekers and skeptics who tend to think of hell as a party waiting to happen or a place of freedom from the supposed constraints of Christianity.

Some might think of heaven as boring, and therefore to be avoided, or as enslavement to God and his will, from which to be emancipated. Still others might despise the Christian God for a variety of reasons, such as a bad run-in with a church, an offputting reading of the Old Testament, or a moral or political disagreement with Christians. Whatever the case, the empty pub analogy provides a clear warning of disappointment to come, of separation from God and his good gifts and isolation from one's fellow human beings.

One time a professor at a campus in California—a Bible professor who was not a Christian—called me out on the notion of hell being essentially the absence of God, which is a C. S. Lewis type of argument.[4] He pointed to some prickly passages in Matthew that seemed to indicate I was underplaying the scenario, that hell was considerably more repressive than what I was suggesting and that, far from "choosing hell for themselves," sinners were sent there by God.

In response, I say okay. Make it even harder. The professor's interpretation of the "hell texts" certainly has a long history in the church and, if true, it should raise the warning flag even higher of tough times to come for those who reject God's offer of salvation in Jesus Christ.

FIVE OBJECTIONS (AND REPLIES) TO THE IDEA OF HELL

I'd like to offer some practical suggestions for conversations with critics around five of the most common objections to the doctrine of hell.

1. But does hell really exist? Reply: If Jesus believed in hell, I should as well. In the Gospels he talks about it quite a bit, especially in Matthew, always in terms of a warning, a place you don't want to go. For the skeptic, I try to contextualize the doctrine of hell into the Big Story (see chapter seven). It needs to fit into a larger schematic or it seems to be an arbitrary and isolated doctrine designed to scare people. Rather, hell fits logically into the overall picture of Christianity: it represents the ultimate consequence of human rejection of God, both as God's justice in condemning sin and in God's respect of human free will to reject him permanently.

For the person still needing to establish the reliability of the biblical accounts of Jesus before adopting Jesus' views on hell, see chapter five and the suggested resources listed there.

2. Hasn't the idea of hell been used as a tool of manipulation and fear? At times, yes. Hellfire-and-brimstone preaching can be used to guilt people into professions of false faith, and sometimes authority figures have held out the threat of hell as a way to coerce moral behavior. Let us distance ourselves from such practices. I'm reminded of the sermon of terror inflicted upon the boy, Stephen Dedalus, in James Joyce's *Portrait of an Artist as a Young Man:*

> My dear boys . . . in earthly prisons the poor captive has at least some liberty of movement . . . not so in hell. There, by reason of the great number of the damned, the prisoners are heaped together in their awful prison, the walls of which are said to be four thousand miles thick: and the damned are so utterly bound and helpless that . . . they are not even able to remove from the eye a worm that gnaws it.[5]

This approach fulfills negative stereotypes but represents only a small fraction of teaching in the church about hell. Unfortunately, skeptics tend to seize upon such "worst practices" and play them up as normative. I figure I've heard more than two thousand sermons in my life in maybe three hundred settings (I get around!), and almost none have been of this variety. Whenever hell is the main subject, sermons tend to offer simple and solemn warnings, such as those I gave my children years ago about not playing with fire.

3. Where's my choice? Skeptics sometimes complain that God doesn't offer any viable choices. It's either believe in him or go to hell. Where's the "free will" in that?

Again, all the issues surrounding hell must be taken in light of the whole story of the Bible. God created us for relationship with him. That's his intention and prerogative, and he knows that if we choose this relationship, we'll flourish as human beings. But when we decline the relationship and instead serve ourselves, God lets go. This is the lesson of Romans 1:24-28, where Paul uses the phrase "God gave them over" three times to indicate God's release of rebellious human beings to their own devices, which is a foretaste of hell. George Bernard Shaw said, "Hell is where you must do what you want to do."[6]

For the skeptic, then, the supposed absence of choice really is a choice: not God's way or the highway—rather, God's way or *your* way. Choose wisely.

4. *Eternal punishment doesn't "fit" the crime*. We hear a lot about God's justice, but is it really "just" for God to condemn a person to eternal punishment for only a few decades of earthly sin? Like the death penalty for stealing a loaf of bread?

One response is that there's no indication, scripturally or logically, that a person's sin is complete when her earthly life is over. In his essay "Heaven and Hell," philosopher Michael Murray reminds us that in hell people continue to sin. They are "maximally set in their ways" owing to deeply ingrained patterns established in their mortal lives. Thus the penalties for sin continue to mount and are never satisfied.[7]

Additionally, the conservative theologian John Walvoord notes, "If the slightest sin is infinite in its significance, then it also demands infinite punishment as a divine judgment."[8] Sinning against God has eternal significance—and consequences. Only human arrogance could possibly demand that God adhere to human standards. One thinks of Job's protests against God, which are answered with, "Will the one who contends with the Almighty correct him?" (Job 40:2).

Finally, we could say that, yes, the consequences of rejecting God are eternal, but you're getting what you want, supposedly. It's like the drunk who wishes to be left alone with his bottle. He's happy now, he thinks, though everyone around him can see how pathetic his condition really is. That's hell. That's the incredibly small world of the empty pub. Of the damned we may say, "God allows them to become eternalized in their self-creation."[9]

5. *God is love. He wouldn't send people to hell*. Sorry if I sound like a broken record, but the God-of-love argument needs to be set into the larger grid of Christian theology. The best place to do this is at the cross, which is the seat of an astonishing paradox between

God's justice and love: sin is so objectionable to God that he went to ultimate lengths to deal with it, sacrificing his only Son. That's the justice of God as he "pours out his wrath" on sin. Paradoxically, God so loved the world that he gave his only Son for our sake (see John 3:16). At the cross, then, justice and love are fused together in the person of Jesus Christ.

THE POWER OF AN IMAGE

I like the image of hell as an empty pub because it works for older skeptics who may have frequented bars and pubs for decades but also younger generations who are huge into community and loathe the idea of being alone. I remember giving a talk at Central Michigan University on the problem of suffering and evil in light of a God who is good and all-powerful. During the Q&A time we ended up talking about God's justice, and then we were into the doctrine of hell. Hell is like an empty pub, I suggested, and then went on to explain what that implies about community, relationships and isolation.

A year later, I was back at CMU, talking with a student named Cheri in the University Cup coffee shop. She reminded me of that talk from twelve months earlier, particularly the part about hell. She said it got her started on a renewed pathway of faith, one of relationship with God and with the people of God. I had no idea she'd been present and had even forgotten that I'd given that particular talk. But it shows the convincing power of a clear image.

CLOSING THOUGHT

An empty pub cannot be the stopping point for our explanations about hell. It's an experiential image that carriers a lot of emotional freight, but it needs additional data, such as theological material (see #5 above) and specific biblical references, to fill out a more complete picture.[10]

SUGGESTED RESOURCES

William Crockett, ed., *Four Views on Hell* (Grand Rapids, MI: Zondervan, 1996).

C. S. Lewis, *The Great Divorce*, new ed. (New York: HarperOne, 2009).

Michael J. Murray, "Heaven and Hell," in *Reason for the Hope Within* (Grand Rapids, MI: Eerdmans, 1993).

PART THREE
SCIENCE AND FAITH

12

ELEPHANT TRAPS

And other
Images for Science and Faith

THAT SLIM, MIDDLE-AGED FELLOW you see standing in front of about fifty students in the student union at Big Campus in the Midwest is me. You may notice the knees knocking a bit, a tremor in the voice, hesitation in the eyes. All this bodily quivering is due to a small platoon of atheists in the audience who are applying a religion-is-stupid, science-is-everything full-court press against me. Maybe I should have just done straight lecture this evening and not taken any questions. Too late now.

As you listen to the atheists' arguments, something doesn't sound quite right. You're not sure what it is. What you're sure of, however, is the confidence—possibly even arrogance—of their manner and the rhetorical force of their points. The one named Justin points a finger at me, asserting, "The creation accounts in the Bible are fairy tales. I defy you to show me a shred of scientific evidence that they're true! Evolution has been proved over and over. Why should I believe the Bible, which is taken on pure faith, when science can give me some real facts?"

Justin's case sounds convincing on the surface but you suspect flaws underneath. Unfortunately, he's got you a little flustered; you can't think clearly. You're hoping the Minnesotan up front will come through with something brilliant, but frankly, you doubt it will happen. As well you should. There was a time when my response in high-pressure situations like this consisted of abstract, on-the-fly arguments that probably no one understood in the moment—or remembered later (including me).

But how nice it would be to have some concrete, pre-planned images to lay down without having to think about it too hard. That's the new me, and I hope you'll join me in this practical approach.

SCIENCE'S MAIN OBJECTION TO GOD

We begin with a summary statement of the typical objections to God from atheists who think science and faith are in competition with each other. Atheist philosopher Thomas Nagel has said, "One of the things atheists tend to believe is that modern science is on their side. . . . Faith as a basis of belief is inconsistent with the scientific conception of knowledge."[1] So if a person is really committed to science and the scientific method, faith will be excluded. This basic premise serves as a launching pad for all sorts of verdicts against faith: that it traffics in ignorance and superstition, that its god(s) are superfluous in explaining the origin and development of life, that it doesn't provide "real" knowledge of the world, that it must necessarily recede and vanish as science progresses.

The counter images I suggest are these: elephant traps, the novelist, the bricklayer, the shrinking island and the smoking gun.

NO "SCIENTIFIC" EVIDENCE FOR GOD? ELEPHANT TRAPS

I use the elephant trap image whenever I encounter what's called the "presumption of atheism." In an essay by that title, atheist philosopher Antony Flew made the point that atheism is innocent until proven guilty. And it is up to theism to prove that God exists. Think of a court of law where the defendant—atheism—is presumed innocent until proven guilty by the prosecution—theism. In support of this, atheists sometimes say, "Whoever makes the statement that something exists must make their case." So according to Flew, if I say that the abominable snowman exists, the burden of proof is on me; the ball is in my court to provide evidence to back up my claim.

Furthermore, modern skeptics have added to Flew's premise by asserting that only one kind of evidence can be brought against atheism in this court of law: scientific evidence. Thus Richard Dawkins says, "The presence or absence of a creative super-intelligence is unequivocally a scientific question."[2] The reason atheists restrict admissible evidence in this fashion is that they assume a simple truth: science is all we've got. If you can't show the existence of some object or being—such as the Loch Ness monster or God—by the use of the scientific method, then your claim is meaningless or false.

In reply, I say that this science-only approach is like setting out mousetraps to catch elephants. After a couple of days you walk around to inspect your mousetraps, and upon finding no elephants you declare that elephants don't exist. That's absurd. If you want to catch elephants, you have to use elephant traps. Science is simply the wrong tool for the job. It's the wrong way to "trap," or detect, God. (In fact, it's also the wrong tool for capturing other things that are not scientifically measurable but are nonetheless real, such as justice, love, loyalty and meaning.)

Now is where we must be careful not to overplay our hand. When we say that science is the wrong tool for the job, we're saying that empirical science by itself will not observe God directly. That is, you can't put God under a microscope or record his voice or touch his shoulder or make a video of his movements. And since it's that narrow range of data that the atheist typically means by "scientific evidence," the elephant trap analogy works well.

But we should also be thinking to ourselves at this point, and perhaps saying aloud in conversation, that science is, in fact, helpful in detecting God, for we see his effects in the existence and design of the universe (see chapters three and four). And if we are going to "play our whole orchestra" of apologetic material, we will include our observations of the universe in making our case for God.

To further the conversation with my atheist friend, I would ask these three questions:

- What if God isn't the sort of being who is directly observable by science?

- What if God has revealed himself to us in other ways?

- What if God asks us to discover him on his terms rather than ours?

If the implied answers to these questions are true—namely, that God is not directly observable, that he has in fact revealed himself to us in other ways, and that he invites us to himself on his terms rather than ours—science-only skeptics would miss the truth. They would fail to find God, even though God is very much there for the finding. At this point, then, we need to be ready to offer some positive reasons for belief in God, such as those from cosmology, design, experience, morality and the historical Jesus.

I used the elephant trap analogy at a Wisconsin campus in conversation with Sean, an avowed skeptic. In essence, I was asking him to open his mind to the possibility of widening the range of "admissible evidence" in his internal court of law. He said he'd consider it.

As you interact with atheists and other skeptics, remember that the road to God (or back to God) is often slow going for them. Sean did ask me for a summer reading list, which I took to be a step in the right direction.

LAWS OF NATURE ARE UNBREAKABLE? THE NOVELIST

Imagine a novelist who creates a world with its own unique properties. My wife Sharon and I are watching the Harry Potter movies these days, a perfect example of world-making with internal rules to which the characters must adhere. These "rules," or what we might call laws of nature, were set up by author J. K. Rowling to include the phenomenon of magic and many other wonders not experienced (that I know of) here in Minnesota.

Now suppose the Harry Potter characters begin to say something like this: "Our world is a closed system. The laws of nature are the bottom line. No breaking of the laws of nature is possible. That's why they're called laws!"

But of course Rowling, the novelist, being the creator of said laws, can tweak and intervene and tinker with or even rewrite the laws if she wishes. The laws are only unbreakable in a closed system (that is, a system that's not open to being changed from the outside). But if the system is open, as in a novel, what's to prevent the creator of the universe, the author, from stepping in at any time and messing with the system? In fact, I'm guessing Rowling rewrote the script many times before publication.

An even sharper example is the Will Ferrell character Harold Crick in the movie *Stranger Than Fiction*. Crick does in fact get in contact with his "novelist," Karen Eiffel (played by Emma Thompson), in order to influence her into writing a happy ending to his life. Crick knows that the narrative of his days on earth is open to reordering from the one who is essentially the "God" figure in the movie—Eiffel.

The idea here is to suggest to science-only skeptics that the laws of nature operate without exception only in a closed system. But why assume we live in a closed system? How would a person know that? Just as the characters in a story may not "know" about their own novelist—in fact, may deny she exists at all—so the characters in the human drama may attempt in vain to deny the Novelist of their own story line, thus ruling out miracles and the existence of God.

So the novelist analogy is not really an argument for God's existence or even the insufficiency of the laws of nature. It's merely an invitation for the skeptic to reconsider a powerful vision: What if we live in an "open" universe in which God can intervene?

NO SUPERNATURAL REALM? THE BRICKLAYER

One of my friends, Bob, is a bricklayer by trade. I'm told it's quite an art, that guys like me with no training shouldn't run out and start throwing together brick homes and retaining walls and staircases as though we're living in adult Legoland. Bob also plays the French horn—yes, a man of many talents. But for all his skills, would I want him doing my taxes? Repairing my car? Working on my teeth?

Probably not. I can tell you for sure, he's no dentist. Bob is wise enough to stick with his specialty of masonry and keep his fingers out of people's mouths.

Seems obvious enough, but not in the case of science-only skeptics. They say the natural realm is all there is, that there is no supernatural realm. The late Carl Sagan is famous for his statement "The cosmos is all there is or ever was or ever will be." The backdrop for such statements is philosophical naturalism, as mentioned above.

But think about it: Science is good at discovering and predicting natural phenomena. You could draw a square on a piece of paper and write "natural world" inside. That's the realm of science. But the moment science presumes to tell us what's outside the square, it's gone beyond its specialty. Now science is doing philosophy— making claims about the fundamental nature of reality and knowledge. The bricklayer is doing dental work.

And what do science-only skeptics tell us is outside the square? Nothing. There is no "outside" the square, they say. There is no supernatural realm and therefore no being called God.

But you have to wonder how science knows this. How can a discipline designed to study the natural realm (inside the square) make pronouncements about a possible supernatural realm (outside the square)? Better to check in with the philosophers and theologians on this question. Similarly, if I want to learn about cavities and root canals, I'll check with my dentist rather than Bob.

I am one of science's biggest supporters. I say thank you, science, for giving me the gifts of central heating here in the northland, of a cell phone, of aspirin, of the weather forecast. Just don't fall into arrogance. Don't start thinking you're an expert on everything. In fact, consider the reverse situation: Would you want philosophers predicting hurricanes? Theologians disposing of nuclear waste?

So that's the bricklayer analogy. Use it whenever science seems to wander outside its area of expertise.

THE UNIVERSE FULLY EXPLAINED WITHOUT GOD: THE SHRINKING ISLAND

Start roaming the Internet these days and it's not hard to find references to a correlation between the expansion of science and the shrinking of God. To the degree that science goes up, God goes down. The claim is clear: We now have natural explanations for things. Supernatural explanations are no longer needed. Here's a sample from NBC news online: "Sean Carroll, a theoretical cosmologist at the California Institute of Technology, says there's good reason to think science will ultimately arrive at a complete understanding of the universe that leaves no grounds for God whatsoever."[3]

Consider the analogy of the shrinking island. The island represents God. The lake surrounding the island represents science. With every advance in science, the lake rises and the island shrinks. God is losing ground, and as science gets closer to a full explanation of the universe in terms of natural law, the end of God draws near. Perhaps a few desperate treetops of the island remain before it is totally engulfed.

But this picture is false. In our analogy the island represents *ignorance*, not God. God is the one who's actually given the gift of science to humanity in order that our knowledge of the world might increase. He says, in effect, "Have at it! Explore the world; search out its secrets. Celebrate the exciting wonders of the created order." God sends gifted scientists, many of whom are Christians, into subdisciplines such as geology, biology and chemistry armed with a burning passion to unlock the secrets of the cosmos and make the fallen world a better place to inhabit. Done rightly, such investigation will lead to worship as God's "eternal power and divine nature" are observed through the glory of what he has made (Romans 1:20).

So the cool part of this analogy is that the secular mindset (and often the Christian mindset) tracks naturally with your setup of the lake representing science and the island representing God. Everyone nods their head when you start to describe the scene. But then, boom, the punch line: the island isn't God, it's ignorance. And God, far from being threatened by science, actually supports it by providing talented personnel capable of making beneficial discoveries. As a Christian, then, I should never fear new frontiers of knowledge, and I should never in my mind place God on the "shrinking island" again.

PARSIMONY: THE SMOKING GUN

I was listening to Richard Dawkins on public radio one day when he made the "parsimony" argument that I sometimes hear on college campuses: simple explanations are to be preferred over complex ones, and the multiplication of causes is to be avoided. Thus when a given phenomenon can be explained by natural law—say, the rise of life forms on earth due to the processes of evolution—it is an unnecessary and superfluous add-on to include God as a causal factor. One cause (evolution) is to be preferred over two (evolution and God).

This preference for simplicity is called "parsimony" by philosophers and scientists, and, indeed, it is a helpful principle for "shaving away" excess baggage from a theory or for cutting away and eliminating a more bulky theory altogether.

To illustrate, let's say I plan to take my Ford SUV to work one morning but find that one of its tires has gone flat. I don't know the cause, but I come up with two theories. The first is that I drove over roofing nails in the alley behind my house. This theory is supported by several lines of evidence: my neighbor is currently shingling his roof, I steered through the alley four times yesterday, and roofing nails have punctured my tires in the past. Seems a reasonable theory.

The second theory is more complex: A broken bottle must have found its way into the path of my vehicle when I returned from a movie last night. The evidence? My neighbors four doors down were still partying when I arrived home. How did a bottle get transported from the party to my place a half-block away? Probably it was left on someone's back bumper and it slipped off and shattered as he rounded the curve past my driveway. Where is the broken bottle now? No doubt that same neighbor got up early this morning and rushed over to my place, discreetly sweeping up the glass before I noticed anything. How did he see the broken glass from his place four houses away? A few weeks ago he got a new telescope for his birthday. Why would he be using the telescope to look at my driveway? Birds. He loves to bird-watch, and there's a new family of cardinals flying around my yard these days. They're especially active in the early morning hours.

Parsimony prefers the simpler theory (the roofing nails) and is also known as "Occam's razor" after the fourteenth-century thinker William of Occam. The razor is a tool of philosophy and science that cuts between two rival theories, or "shaves away" unnecessary assumptions and causes. Thus you may hear a skeptic say something like the following: "When you've got science you don't need God. Occam's razor dictates that the simpler explanation is to be preferred." Indeed, a professor at Macalester College in St. Paul, Minnesota, once remarked to me that natural law is sufficient to explain most phenomena we observe, so why complicate the picture by adding some sort of supernature?

Here I want to be a little cautious in how I proceed. There is, after all, a sense in which I can agree with the atheistic account of things. A pencil rolls off a desk and falls to the ground. The atheist identifies gravity as the causal factor, then looks at me suspiciously. But I only nod my head: "Yeah, I'm with you. Gravity." I might also be thinking to myself that God created this law of gravity, but, really, there's no need to be contentious in such simple matters.

But say a mutual friend makes a miraculous recovery from sickness. Or a world comes into being out of "nothing" and seems to exhibit beneficial order. Again, an atheist friend identifies natural law as the cause of these things, even though he can't explain all that's involved. And he uses the words "parsimony" or "Occam's razor" to support his position, as if that settles the matter completely.

I say not so fast. I haven't agreed to the idea of parsimony as an unwavering rule for every situation, even though it's often helpful. Here's where the smoking gun analogy comes in.

Let's say Smith is found at the scene of a murder with a smoking gun in his hand. Occam's razor (or parsimony) hastily applied would conclude that Smith is guilty of the crime and would send him to prison (or worse). As it turns out, however, Smith actually came upon the scene shortly after the crime was committed and picked up the gun merely to examine it. He was innocent all the way. The scene was more complicated than first appeared.

One thing to know about parsimony is that simplicity must be balanced with adequacy. Yes, it may be simpler to say that Smith is the murderer. But simple explanations are not always true explanations. In fact, they're often inadequate to fit the details of a particular case. Sometimes there is more to the story than meets the eye.

Besides, who said that naturalistic explanations are always simpler than theistic explanations? What makes a theistic explanation necessarily complicated? God acts; things happen. It's hard to see how that's so much more complex than nature acts; things happen.

So there are two responses we can give to the parsimony argument. One is that sometimes the simplest of explanations is not always the true explanation. This is where the smoking gun analogy is useful. The other is that God explanations are not necessarily more complex than nature explanations. Yes, we ought to be cautious in invoking God as a direct causal force in everyday situations (okay, gravity caused the pencil to fall), but when it comes to special cases such as miracles and world making, saying that "God did it" is both rational and simple.

A REAL-LIFE CONVERSATION

Let me share an encounter I had with Sandy, a PhD student at a campus in the Midwest, that illustrates some of the points made above. Sandy attended one of my outreach talks, offered an intelligent objection during the Q&A time at the end, listened carefully to my reply, and scheduled lunch with me the next day through a mutual friend.

Lunch consisted of deli food in the student union. Sandy began by thanking me for my respectful response to another student who'd spoken quite forcefully the evening before. I thanked God silently that I'd shown some grace. My darker side had been a real possibility. Note to self: Rick, your manner is just as important as your words. Tone of voice is louder than logic. Resist the temptation to match your opponent's combative posture with same.

Then suddenly we were into it. I learned quickly that Sandy was all about proving things. She began with a lengthy frame-up of two opposing worlds—one of science, facts and proofs and the other of religion and faith. The first world gives us real knowledge that is reliable, testable, verifiable. The second gives literally nothing except subjective speculation. One might as well say something absurd, such as "God has a big tongue," as say anything at all about God. Any talk about God is literally meaningless. "God is love" is not testable scientifically and so doesn't really count for anything in the material world.

Toward the end of this first point from Sandy I reminded myself that I'm supposed to be good at this stuff, so I should be able to defeat her arguments with a few incisive analogies and images. Of

course it's never that easy. She had me a little off-balance. I also
reminded myself to simply care about this fine person who is made
in the image of God.

The dialogue moved forward. Instead of parrying her thrust directly on the grounds she chose (science, provability), I decided to
take the argument to a different location: my ground. I told my
story, my version of the world. I set up a competing universe that
made sense in its own right, even if it didn't make sense to Sandy
(for the moment). My universe, I explained, is like a novel—open
to reordering from the outside by the novelist.

Sandy replied that any assertions about said novelist were un-
provable and therefore worthless—unless they had some practical
value such as providing emotional comfort or a basis for morality.
But God talk itself couldn't be "true" in the normal sense of the word.

Put yourself in my place. What's your next move? (And how can
you speak in a winsome tone that prevents this encounter from
devolving into a verbal fistfight?)

I think you can go two ways. One is elephant traps: science—as
narrowly construed by Sandy—is the wrong tool for the job. Hey, if
you want to catch elephants, use elephant traps, not mousetraps.
Or you could go with the bricklayer. That's what I did. I gently
pointed out to Sandy that she was making philosophical statements,
not scientific ones. She was expressing a philosophical preference
for "proofs," and this preference itself was not scientifically provable.
She was acting like the proverbial bricklayer who leaves behind his
true profession to try his hand at dental work.

Sandy listened intently without blinking.

Furthermore, I said, proof is an extremely difficult standard to
meet in most areas of life. Does her family love her? Did she have
eggs for breakfast? Was George Washington an actual historical
figure? Did America put a man on the moon? Will her car take her
home safely later this evening? There is plenty of evidence for all
these matters, but proving them is tougher than one might think.

This last point is critical because as much as science-only folks want to live by the science-only credo, usually they can't keep it up across the board. At best, they can admit that science hangs in the background—and that if forced, time allowing, they could bring the scientific method to the foreground by doing the necessary research on each item to come up with a proof of sorts. But no one is truly motivated for this kind of legwork. Yet they live on, assuming as true lots of things without any proof whatsoever.

So the inconsistent application of the scientific method across one's life is a point I often try to make with skeptics. Some of life is "scientific," other parts not so much. I've yet to hear a thoughtful justification for this uneven application of the scientific method. And even if such a justification is out there, ninety-nine percent of the skeptics you encounter don't know about it or can't articulate it anyway.

I'll close this story by reminding you and myself that many of the images and analogies I'm offering up in this book may look like slam dunks on paper, but in live settings it's rarely so easy. Often I can't even discern the precise objection a skeptic is making. Few express themselves clearly and lucidly. So I end up fishing around for awhile, poking here and there, asking questions until I figure out exactly what they're saying. Sandy, for example, was equating "proofs" with science, which seems obvious now in the retelling. I didn't catch it at first, but when I did, novelist and bricklayer came to the rescue.

Postscript: Six months after this conversation, I checked in with one of the campus workers who was following up with Sandy. The report was good. Sandy was asking more questions, making progress and, most importantly, feeling loved and accepted by the Christian community.

CHAPTER SUMMARY

The underlying idea of this chapter is that when science operates in its legitimate domain—that of studying the natural world—everything is fine. Christians should love science! And it is a point of fact that many Christians go into various fields of science and thrive there as students and professionals. It's only when science grows arrogant and begins to make dogmatic statements about philosophy and theology that Christians must object, perhaps using the images suggested above. To review, then:

When Science Says This	Use This Image
There is no scientific evidence for God. Therefore God doesn't exist.	Elephant traps: That's like setting out mousetraps to catch elephants. Wrong tool for the job. You need elephant traps.
The laws of nature are unbreakable.	The novelist: But that's only in a closed system. If the system is open, as in a novel, the novelist can intervene whenever she wishes.
The natural realm is all there is. There is no supernatural realm.	The bricklayer: That's not science, it's philosophy. Would you want a bricklayer doing your dental work? Science should stick to science and not presume to know things outside its domain.
Science is providing natural explanations for everything. God is no longer needed.	The shrinking island: God is not merely an explanation but a real being. We tend to think of science as a lake that gradually rises to overcome an ever-shrinking island called God. But in reality, the island is ignorance, and God is the one who's raising the lake (science) by sending the rain (gifted scientists).
Parsimony (Occam's razor) dictates that the simpler of explanations is always preferred. Adding God to natural explanations is an unnecessary complication.	The smoking gun: Simpler explanations are not always accurate. If Smith is found over a dead body with a smoking gun in hand, it doesn't necessarily mean he committed the murder. Additionally, who says that God is necessarily a more complex explanation for things? "God did it" is just as simple as "Nature did it."

SUGGESTED RESOURCES

J. P. Moreland, ed., *The Creation Hypothesis* (Downers Grove, IL: Inter-Varsity Press, 1994), especially chap. 1.

Alvin Plantinga, *Where the Conflict Really Lies: Science, Religion, and Naturalism* (New York: Oxford University Press, 2011).

C. Stephen Evans and R. Zachary Manis, *Philosophy of Religion: Thinking About Faith*, 2nd ed. (Downers Grove, IL: IVP Academic, 2009), chap. 6.

13

MIRACLES ARE LIKE A HOLE IN ONE

IN THE GAME OF GOLF, the chances of the average player making a hole in one are around twelve thousand to one.[1] Even at those odds, it's not uncommon for folks who play very little golf to score an "ace" (another term for a hole in one). Recently I heard of a guy who even accomplished the feat the very first time he played.

Contrast that with me, the hardcore golfer. I've labored at the game my whole life—maybe three thousand rounds' worth, which equates to about fifteen thousand hole in one chances—and never had an ace. The point is that holes in one are unusual but not impossible. And the rarity of the feat is the angle we'll use later in the chapter to make an important point about miracles.

DEFINING AWAY MIRACLES

The perpetual smirk that showed on Joey's face whenever he was around Christians seemed to say, "I know I'm smarter than you. You could never out-argue me; don't even try." It was a look of superiority. Cold gray eyes and a smug manner added to the disagreeable effect. Not a pleasant character to hang out with.

But hang out we did. One afternoon in the student union of a college in the Midwest, a Christian student and I had a two-hour conversation with Joey. The deeper we got into the issues surrounding his atheism, the more he seemed to let down his guard. Underneath the smirk-and-smug was a decent fellow who was allowing us to see a different side of his personality, including a measure of vulnerability and grace. But then we came to the topic of miracles. Joey's position was this:

1. The natural realm is all there is.

2. Miracles don't fit in the natural realm.

3. Therefore miracles don't occur.

Joey was simply trying to define miracles out of existence. This way of thinking is usually based on what skeptics call a "scientific" understanding of the universe. But the first thing to notice about statement number one is that it's not scientific at all, but rather philosophical. Scientific statements sound like this: "The speed of light is x." "The size of the galaxy is y." Scientific statements usually refer to phenomena that are observable, testable and repeatable, but number one is none of these. Rather, it amounts to a gigantic philosophical claim and is highly debatable (see chapter twelve for more).

When we pointed this out to Joey, it didn't register. He didn't understand what we were driving at. His whole life was based on science, he insisted, so "the natural realm is all there is" seemed to him a logical statement. I asked how he could put the claim "the natural realm is all there is" to a scientific test—that is, how could it be observable, testable, repeatable? Blank stare. The cold eyes now penetrated my forehead. Gone was the warmth of a moment ago. We were done for the day.

Many other thoughtful skeptics, however, know that the skeptic's argument (numbers one through three) doesn't hold water by itself, so they dig deeper, often relying on the case against miracles made by the eighteenth-century Scottish philosopher David Hume. Hume's writings are sophisticated and witty, and I count myself among his admirers—not that I agree with him. If we are able to respond thoughtfully to Hume, we'll be a long way toward responding well to many contemporary skeptics' objections to miracles.

HUME'S CASE AGAINST MIRACLES

In theory, Hume allows for the possibility of miracles, but in practice he pretty much eliminates them from serious consideration. That's because none of the reports about miracles, even from eyewitnesses, can be believed, he says. Why? To summarize: Such reports always come from people who are either deceived or deceivers. Either they misperceive the event in question or they deliberately invent tall tales to share with gullible listeners who are all too eager to believe. It's human nature to be infatuated with the extraordinary, the unusual—rich soil for false belief.

So one could rightly believe in a miracle if there were credible evidence, but Hume draws the rules of "credible evidence" such that no credible evidence is ever possible. Furthermore, for Hume, the regularities of natural law have a cumulative effect that counts decisively against miracles. You have to "add up" all the times the world behaves normally and compare them with the number of supposed violations of natural law. Normal behavior wins every time.[2]

For example, Joshua 10:12-13 records the account of Joshua asking the Lord for the sun to stand still, which it does, delaying its setting "about a full day." Were Hume to comment, he'd likely point out how many times the sun has risen and set on its normal schedule since the beginning of time. Then he'd subtract all these occurrences from the authority and credibility of the miracle claim. After such a massive subtraction, Joshua's suspended sun completely vanishes as a plausible event. If Hume were to speak from the grave, he might say, "What's more sensible to the enlightened person: that the solar system continued its habitual movements as it has from time immemorial, or that an ancient barbarian convinced his god to run it off course for a day? Stop with the superstition!"

So, to summarize where we've come so far: Some skeptics, such as Joey, define miracles out of existence merely by stating that the natural realm is all there is. Other skeptics dig deeper and follow David Hume's attack: that reports of miracles are simply not believable due to the unreliability of witnesses, and that evidence from our constant experience of the "normal operations" of nature overwhelm the evidence for miracles.

How can Christians respond in a thoughtful manner?

AN IMAGE FOR CONVERSATION: A HOLE IN ONE

A hole in one is a helpful analogy for the topic of miracles because it shows the danger of being closed to possibilities. Here's a short parable to illustrate: Jim is an ardent skeptic who believes in natural law and the unreliability of all miracle reports. He has a wonderful daughter, Ashley, whom he loves with all his heart. At age nine she goes to a local golf course with a neighbor girl and plays golf for the first time in her life. Returning home afterward, she's elated, reporting excitedly to her father that she got a hole in one on a 175-yard hole (which is pretty long, especially for a young girl).

What's Jim to believe? His heart tells him to accept the report as true so he can celebrate with Ashley. But his mind remains skeptical. He checks out the story with the neighbor girl. She tells it exactly like Ashley did. Perhaps they're mistaken. Perhaps a squirrel ran it into the hole. No, that would be even more staggering. Maybe they miscounted the score; maybe this is a schoolgirl prank; maybe Ashley lost her ball and found someone else's in the hole. He concocts fifty explanations. He smiles and gives Ashley a big hug and pretends to bond with his daughter over her amazing feat. But secretly Jim doesn't believe it really happened. He can't.

As the narrator of this parable I can tell you that Ashley did in fact make an ace. Unfortunately, Jim's prior assumptions about how the world works prevent him from recognizing the truth. Let's uncover Jim's prior assumptions: First, holes in one are extremely rare, even for experienced golfers who've played the game their whole lives. Second, golfers are prone to exaggerate their feats. They love to tell tall tales about their golfing prowess. This opens the door wide to false testimony. Third, nine-year-old girls simply do not make holes in one their first time playing golf. Take all the nine-year-old girls in history who did not make an ace their first time out, add the sum total of these "normal experiences" together, and stack them up against the claim that one girl did make an ace. The one exception is overwhelmed by the normality of the many. Ergo, it's more sensible to disbelieve, even if it's your own daughter.

Now I ask, why would anyone want to hold a view of the world that at times actually *prevents* them from believing the truth? That's what Jim is doing.

As an experiment, let's see how Jim's worldview holds up under pressure. Let's say his three prior assumptions, named above, are still firmly in place. And let's say that he's the sort of person who takes a certain pride in being objective and sensible in his judgments, avoiding superstitions and believing in the eventual triumph of rational, scientific explanations for anomalous events such as miracles.

In order to test Jim's worldview under pressure, let's change the script by placing him at the scene as an eyewitness. In this position he observes firsthand the unlikely ace scored by his lovely daughter. As the ball rolls on to the green and disappears into the cup, he leaps in the air and twists with a loud shriek. He grabs the sky. He cries with joy. He gives Ashley a joyous massive bear hug.

But does he believe?

Similarly, let's put David Hume into the scene of Joshua 10. Hume observes the sun standing still for a day. He thinks to himself, "This can't be happening."

I think there are two ways these scenes can play out. One is that Jim and Hume stick to their principles and deny what they're seeing. After all, they're still bound to the idea that millions of events functioning "normally" according to the laws of nature will outweigh and defeat any weird claims to the contrary. And since they inherently don't trust eyewitnesses, they must refrain from trusting themselves. That's taking the high road, absurd as it sounds.

Alternatively, they could recognize the folly of their assumptions and embrace the ace and believe in the extended sunshine.

The choice seems easy, doesn't it?

Not to everyone. Not, for example, to certain folks on college campuses who insist that they're among the most committed to rational thought of anyone. I once met a student at a junior college in California who was, as I like to say, science all the way. I found Derrick to be friendly, engaging and smart. I asked him if he believed in God and he said no, citing science and natural law as his guides to true knowledge. Then I asked if he believes in miracles. No, same reasons. Next I asked how he'd respond if he witnessed a miracle firsthand or if God appeared to him in person. Without hesitation Derrick said that the probability of himself hallucinating was greater than the probability that God and miracles exist, so no, he would still not believe.

Finally, a colleague of mine who was listening to our conversation asked Derrick what he thought of Christians who held to their beliefs blindly and refused to open their minds to the possibility of being wrong. "I have no respect for them," Derrick replied.

Seeing an opening, my colleague threw down the clincher: "Derrick, don't you see how you're doing the same thing? Doesn't it bother you that you're just as closed-minded as the Christians you don't respect?"

To Derrick's credit, he admitted that, yes, it did bother him. But he didn't know what to do about it. He was one hundred percent committed to his worldview and wasn't going to change. As C. S. Lewis points out in his "Miracles" essay, "Whatever experiences we may have, we shall not regard them as miraculous if we already hold a philosophy which excludes the supernatural."[3]

Another time I asked my friend Professor West at Macalester

College in St. Paul what he'd think if Jesus appeared to him in person. Now retired, Dr. West was at the time a popular philosophy professor at the school and openly atheistic. "I'd find a way to explain it away as a hallucination," was his answer.

Yikes. That cheering you hear in the background is David Hume from the grave, exhorting his philosophical descendants to stay the course and not allow dumb stuff like direct experience with miracles (and little girls' aces) to overturn their commitment to rational thinking.

And that yelling you hear in the foreground is me dressing down the Scottish philosopher: "Mr. Hume, I love your writings! You're clever and funny! But I gotta tell you, there's a dude here named Jim who just missed a once-in-a-lifetime event with his beautiful daughter because he was wearing the blinders you gave him. What do you say to that?"

THE SKEPTIC'S REPLY

If you employ the hole in one analogy in a conversation with a skeptic who's "science all the way," she's likely to reply that the analogy doesn't hold. A hole in one is not a supernatural event, she'll say, and therefore not a violation of natural law. Sure, it's unusual. Unusual stuff happens all the time. No big deal. But violations of natural law don't happen. The analogy is flawed.

Now's when you need to hold your ground. The hole in one analogy works because it suggests that if a person used David Hume's argument consistently, she would reject every unusual event. But it's unreasonable to reject every unusual event, because they do in fact occur. Therefore Hume's argument is unreasonable. We need to examine the evidence for each incident in question and simply ask, "Might this be one of those unusual events (a miracle, a rare hole in one) or not?" It must be judged on its own merits, not reinterpreted through the filter of prior assumptions.

Suppose ten sane, reliable witnesses see a demon exorcised from a person who's suddenly healed of his affliction and restored to his right mind. Or ten sane, reliable witnesses give independent confirming testimony of a single person removing an automobile off a victim pinned underneath. Will the skeptic believe?

Suppose the skeptic himself witnesses these unusual events. What then? The high road of principled disbelief, which is absurd? Or the humble recognition that anomalies sometimes occur in the regularity of natural law—and that once in a blue moon little girls don't make their usual nines and tens on par threes but rather ones on their maiden voyage around the greens?

PRACTICAL APPLICATION FOR CONVERSATIONS

Okay, here's how things often play out. If you can track with this summary you should be in good position to lay down the hole in one analogy in a real conversation:

1. Skeptic declares that miracles don't happen.

2. You ask for the reasoning behind this statement.

3. Skeptic replies that science proves natural law. Supernatural realm doesn't exist. Therefore, no miracles.

4. You point out that it seems skeptic is simply defining miracles out of existence.

5. Now skeptic takes a Hume-like approach: that miracle reports are always unreliable and that the evidence for a miracle must be weighed against the sum total of all the "normal" events that went before it. Skeptic probably won't put it exactly in those terms, but that's the general drift.

6. You lay down the hole in one analogy.

7. Skeptic objects that holes in one are not supernatural events, so the analogy doesn't work.

8. You reply that all you're doing is showing how skeptic is shutting out the possibility of unusual events of any kind, whether natural or supernatural.

9. Then you place skeptic at the scene. You ask whether he would believe in a miracle if he saw one himself, or if he'd believe in God if God made a personal appearance. If yes, skeptic is being inconsistent with his own principles. If no, he's being absurd.

10. The moral of the story: Assumptions determine conclusions. If a person assumes that miracles and little girls' aces don't happen, their actual occurrence will be missed. Better to be open to possibilities than to be dogmatically committed to a worldview with built-in blind spots.

PART FOUR

HOW-TO'S

14

HOW TO TALK WITH SKEPTICS

An Introduction

UP TO THIS POINT we've been looking at how to use images and analogies to enhance our conversations with seekers and skeptics. You may be wondering, however, how to begin talking with these folks in the first place—how to get beyond topics such as the weather and into spiritual issues.

PEELING AWAY THE LAYERS

The diagram below is how I tend to think of the process of evangelism—let's say with a non-Christian friend named David.

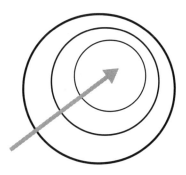

Figure 3.

Actually, the diagram represents David's layers. The outer layer indicates our common interests, such as studies, home and garden, and work. The middle layer represents his opinions and values, the inner circle his basic identity and beliefs. Of course, in real life it's not this neat and clean—the layers overlap and run together quite a bit. Nevertheless, as David and I gradually build a trusting friendship, the layers of both our lives peel away and a deep connection is made. It's a wonderful Holy Spirit adventure. Along the way I'm sharing the gospel message as the Spirit leads, a process that seems to intensify as we get down to the core of each other's lives.

So let's say David lives next door to my house here in St. Paul. Early in our friendship we banter about winter snow removal and other stuff in the external world—his new bike, a sports team, holiday plans. But over time, as our conversations progress beyond the outer layer into values and opinions, it seems we both have more at stake in the relationship. Not that it happens overnight. It may take days or weeks—or years—to establish trust, and it varies with each person. With some folks I just seem to click, and we get down to brass tacks pretty fast. With others, it takes ages. In any case, meaningful friendships require mutual sharing.

In a recent workshop at a church here in the Twin Cities, I presented this same model of evangelism—sometimes called the "onionskin" method—and I challenged participants to become experts at asking questions and getting to know other people. Most heads were nodding. But when I suggested that there needs to be an equal amount of self-disclosure in these relationships—that is, mutual sharing—I sensed resistance in the room. But that's what it takes to connect meaningfully with a friend who's far from God. We have to be willing to let others into our own interior self if we expect the same from them. And it's at this center of identity and belief that the gospel has the most impact and transforming power. So with David, that's where I want to be speaking and praying the message of Christ into his life.

The chart below lists some specific elements you might find in the various layers of a person you're getting to know:

Outer layer	Small talk	Hobbies, work, vacations, weather
Middle layer(s)	Opinions, values	Family, goals, politics, money
Inner layer(s)	Beliefs, identity	Spiritual beliefs, insecurities, family secrets, emotional health, addictions

So that's the basic idea of moving from *out* to *in* in a relationship.

FAQs

I'd like to address some common questions posed by Christians on the topic of personal evangelism, after which we'll focus on distinguishing between "modern" and "postmodern" non-Christians, and why this difference matters.

In this whole process, when do I let on that I'm a Christian? Early and often. Almost everyone in my life knows I'm a Christian, even if they don't know me well. It's good to mention things like church, your pastor or priest, prayer, holiday traditions, authors you're reading—anything that will get God stuff out in the open. Oh, and use humor. Never hurts to poke fun at yourself or your odd family quirks and traditions.

When do I share the gospel? I like to share little parts of it all over the place. That means the gospel has to be an integrated, natural part of my life. I can't be putting on my evangelism hat and then taking it off and then donning it again. No, it's always on, because evangelism is not some foreign activity I do, it's who I am. At least that's the goal. Here's an example of sharing bits of God's truth at each stage:

Outer layer. Sorry, I can't come to the game on Saturday because our church is doing a service project that day.

Middle layer. I know your Mom is sick. Please let her know that I'm praying for her regularly.

Inner layer. God is reaching out to you in this lonely season of your life. He's given you the gift of his Son, Jesus—if you'll take him. Could I tell you the story of how it happened to me?

Why do I have to get to know the person so well before sharing Christ? You don't. You can share the message at any time. But I think you'll find that with a lot of people, trust needs to be established before teachable moments present themselves. In their excellent book *I Once Was Lost*, Doug Schaupp and Don Everts talk about the importance of building trust with non-Christian friends, including learning about them and bonding with them.[1]

I've noticed that my friend Jeff Ballantyne, a skilled evangelist who's led many to Christ, models this approach beautifully. He always seems to know a lot about those who've been coming to faith—their cultural background, interests, hobbies, values, fears. It's because he listens, learns, bonds and shares his life as he shares the gospel. He's interested in others as individuals. In the Gospels, Jesus demonstrates keen interest in the particulars of the lives of the people he meets. He doesn't use the same method with everyone but zeros in on who they really are, whether it's a Pharisee who visits him under cover of darkness, a Samaritan woman with many broken relationships or a young wealthy ruler (see John 3:1-15; 4:4-26; Luke 18:18-24).

Do I have to "go deep" and be best friends with everyone? No. Most of us can maintain only a few close friendships. The way I approach my many non-Christian friends is that I go as deep with them as the Holy Spirit allows. If the other person hasn't been prepared by God to go past the outer layer, then that's where we're at. But with some folks, even if we're not super-close, God opens the door for deep conversations about ultimate issues, and I need to be ready for that at all times. One time at a wedding reception I was seated next to the grandmother of the bride. For whatever reason, we hit it off right away. Fifteen minutes after "hello" she began telling me her life story. And I told her Jesus' life story. In this case, God allowed me to go deep with a stranger.

I'm a private person. I'm not good at relationships. Now what? I have a good friend, Jackie, who's in this boat, and she often feels guilty and deficient. We both know she has a lot to offer, but it's not her natural bent to initiate relationships and "go deep" with others. It's not how she was raised. Two things to mention here. One is that we're all called to be witnesses, if not skilled evangelists, and Jackie is learning how to take risks in relationships, stepping out in faith a little at a time. Adam McHugh, author of *Introverts in the Church*, notes, "So much of me wants to be . . . away from the noise and urgency of other people, but I cannot escape the fact that growth invariably involves the messiness of genuine human contact and the struggles of intimacy."[2] Besides, maybe the person to whom you're reaching out actually needs a quieter, more reflective approach to spirituality than what an outgoing evangelist would provide. Perhaps this is your special calling from the Lord in this person's life.

Secondly, don't forget about the power of community. Maybe your job is simply to invite the person to church or an outreach event and let God speak through other Christians. Remember that witness is a team sport, where the body of Christ brings a multitude of gifts and voices to enable seekers and skeptics to come to faith.[3]

What if the other person has questions or objections regarding Christianity? This is what we want! There are tons of resources in apologetics these days that can help you make a thoughtful response (see the resource list at the end of this chapter and others). In any case, when the other person's questions and objections come out, you know you're connecting significantly with your friend, probably in the middle layers. You might mention, for example, that your pastor has been teaching from the Old Testament. Your friend responds by asking how anyone can believe an ancient book of religion that's been changed and corrupted over the centuries. Now you've really got something to talk about. And pray about.

THE PLACE OF PRAYER

The more I get to know a person, the more informed and targeted my prayers can be. Back to my neighbor David. If I know he's struggling financially, I pray there. If he's hardhearted and stubborn, I pray there. If he's abusing drugs or alcohol or is cheating at school (or on his wife), I pray into those issues.

Overall, I want to be praying for two things: discernment and influence. I need God's help in discerning who David is as a person and what makes him tick. That will dictate how I go about sharing Christ with him. And as our friendship progresses, I'll pray that God will influence David's heart. All my care and service and question answering will do nothing for him without God's Spirit working in his life.[4]

Now let me offer another piece of the puzzle that is crucial to effective witness.

A FORK IN THE ROAD: MODERN OR POSTMODERN?

When I'm first getting to know a non-Christian, sometimes even at the outer layer, there's a specific question I ask myself that has huge implications for my witness to them: is this person mainly modern or postmodern?[5] These are two basic mindsets and they represent a critical fork in the road for our conversations and relationship. I need to determine which of these two directions the person is headed, then intentionally walk alongside them.

We don't even need to get too technical about the history and principles of modernism and postmodernism for the concepts to be helpful.[6] Modernism is the mindset that originated in Europe and North America from roughly the seventeenth century to the present. Postmodernism kicked in somewhere around the 1960s and continues to the present. So there are about forty years of overlap. Often the two ways of doing life are in tension with each other. Here is a sampling of characteristics on each side:

Modern Mindset	Postmodern Mindset[7]
Defining image: a brick	Defining image: a pillow
Logic, reason, rationality	Experience, feelings
Truth	Many truths
Individualism	Groups, community, cooperation
Doing what's right	Doing what works
Science	Humanities
Certainty	Mystery
Power of the majority	Justice for minorities
Progress	Fairness
Give to the poor	Serve the poor
Strong institutions	Cooperative communities
Upwardly mobile	Sidewardly mobile
Excellence	Authenticity
Words, text	Pictures, videos
Lectures, one-way communication	Interactive learning

You can see what a difference it would make in my approach to evangelism if the person was mostly on one side of the ledger or the other. In general terms, moderns need reasons and postmoderns need experiences. Note the defining image for each. Moderns are like bricks. They're firm, clear and have strong foundations. There's nothing squishy about a brick. Postmoderns are like pillows. Throw a rational argument at them and it's likely to be absorbed with minor impact. But walk with them through meaningful experiences and stories and you may see God working deeply in their lives.

If you've ever felt a total disconnect with a non-Christian friend, as if the two of you were on different wavelengths or traveling different roads altogether, maybe it's because you're "moderning" your way through life and she's postmoderning. Or vice versa.

The next two chapters are about how to connect with both camps. We'll also discuss a common modern-postmodern hybrid: a brick in a pillowcase. What would you say to that person?

SUGGESTED RESOURCES

Don Everts and Doug Schaupp, *I Once Was Lost: What Postmodern Skeptics Taught Us About Their Path to Jesus* (Downers Grove, IL: InterVarsity Press, 2008).

Rick Richardson, *Reimagining Evangelism* (Downers Grove, IL: IVP Books, 2006).

Entry-level apologetics: Gregory Boyd, *Letters from a Skeptic*, 2nd ed. (Colorado Springs, CO: David C. Cook, 2008).

Midlevel apologetics: Timothy Keller, *The Reason for God* (New York: Dutton, 2008); Lee Strobel, *The Case for Christ* (Grand Rapids, MI: Zondervan, 1998); Lee Strobel, *The Case for Faith* (Grand Rapids, MI: Zondervan, 2009).

Advanced-level apologetics: Alvin Plantinga, *Where the Conflict Really Lies: Science, Religion, and Naturalism* (New York: Oxford University Press, 2011).

15

HOW TO TALK WITH MODERN SKEPTICS WHO BELIEVE IN GOD

IF I TOLD YOU I WAS RAISED in middle America and am currently over the age of fifty, you might guess I was brought up a modernist, and you'd be right. For twenty-four years (through college) I consumed three square meals a day of rational thinking, belief in a single reality accessible to all, and "absolute truth."

I was a brick. All my foundations were secure. Anyone who couldn't see the same plain truth in front of them that I saw was probably deluded. Common-sense realism was my MO, though spiritually I was but a vague Christian theist. I believed in God, sort of, but was nowhere near an evangelical Christian until my conversion at age nineteen.

In the United States, non-Christians who are modern in their outlook tend to be a little older—at least those who believe in God (atheists, whom I'll cover in the next chapter, span the age spectrum). Modernism is evident in baby boomers and above, while postmodernism is more common among the younger generations. Nevertheless, I meet enough moderns on college campuses to at least temper such generalizations, and we need to account for them as well.

THREE APPROACHES

Whatever the exact demographic trends, the point is that if and when you encounter a modern person, young or old, certain approaches work better than others. Here are three suggestions:

1. *Point to the truth.* Moderns believe in truth, and when they think they might be missing it, even by a little, their conscience kicks in. They wonder if they're thinking properly. Many have an awareness of God, whether it's a vague belief kept on the back burner or something more defined in the front of their minds.

When I ask an interested modern person where the world came from or if the Bible can be trusted or if all religions are the same, he actually cares about "the answer." He's less likely to think these issues are purely relative to one's point of view. Put another way, when a tree falls in the forest, it still makes a sound, even if no one is around to hear it. Why? Because for moderns, there's a real world out there that we can all discuss, and it exists independently of human observers. Thus traditional apologetics that make a case for Christian faith can be very effective—because we're trying to find the truth of the matter.

2. *Point to heaven and hell.* Here is a conversation I had on a lake with one of my older friends, after some bantering about spiritual topics:

"Bruce, how are things with you and God?"

"Still looking for loopholes, Rick. Somehow I have to beat the system, convince the man upstairs to take me in."

"Okay, say you go before the Lord and he asks you why he should let you into heaven. What will you say?"

"I hope I did enough good things in life to outweigh the bad."

"And?"

"I don't know. Could be a close call."

"Had you thought of telling God what you'd done with his Son, Jesus Christ? Whether you'd placed your faith in him?"

"Rick, the fish aren't biting here. Maybe we should move the boat to another spot."

Moderns with a religious sensibility tend to believe we're on a merit system with God. That's the heaven-hell angle. If you're good enough, you're golden. If you're bad—well, we're not sure what happens then. Maybe hell. Maybe something else. Maybe you just die. Hitler, for sure, is in hell. Most moderns have little knowledge of salvation by faith through grace. They are works-oriented, so the idea that you can't save yourself seems very foreign. Older moderns were raised to respect authority, believe in God, put in a hard day's work; they know how the "real world" works: there's no free lunch; you get what you pay for; a penny saved is a penny earned.

A good verse to use with moderns is Ephesians 2:8: "For it is by grace you have been saved, through faith—and this is not from yourselves, it is the gift of God." I like this verse for outreach to moderns because it counters the merit system mentality. Sometimes it's okay to quote it directly, but generally I prefer to paraphrase more casually: "Bruce, the New Testament says that you can't save yourself. Only Christ can do that. You're saved by grace, through faith in Christ. It's a gift—you can't earn it. Nobody can. It's counter-intuitive, I know. But God is the one who gets to make the rules. He's given us his Son. You can accept the gift or not. . . . "

Notice the straight-up references to the Bible, God, the Son and so on. Again, there's a truth out there to which we point, and it culminates in heaven and hell. Many moderns who are not atheists know this, consciously or not, and can be drawn to the light.

I remember attending the funeral of a friend's elderly father a few years ago. Fred had believed in God his whole life and attended church but hadn't accepted the grace of the gospel—until, that is, he moved into a nursing home. There he discovered God's free gift in Christ through talking with his grandchildren. At age eighty-two, he expressed a desire to declare his faith publicly through baptism. Photos at the funeral showed him standing near a lake with head bowed, supported on one arm by my friend, the other arm by the family pastor. Instead of dunking Fred in the lake, however, the pastor poured water on his head from a pitcher. Two years later he died. I cried through the funeral, as I am right now just thinking about it. Sometimes grace wins out over the merit system.

3. Prepare for the unbelief of believers. There are so many ways for moderns to distrust God and the Bible that I am reluctant to narrow it down to a main reason or two. First, being a theist doesn't always solve the problem of distrust. It seems to me that many moderns are skeptical of God—and religion in general—while maintaining belief in God. That's the paradox. Some seem to compartmentalize along these lines: Science has largely replaced God; the church and other religious institutions oppress the masses or are too boring to care about—yet, above and beyond this world, there must be a God. He/She/It is the best explanation for the existence of the universe, and religion plays a role in providing generic moral guidance. Someday I may even be accountable to that God, so I'd better keep it together here on earth.

Secondly, former church attenders are everywhere. Studies from the Pew Foundation show declining religious affiliation among Americans born after the mid-1960s.[1] Add in the church dropout rate for college students and early-twenties folks, and you've got a lot of conversations waiting to happen. Even so, ex-church skepticism is a pretty daunting hurdle to overcome. Simply asking, "What went wrong? What caused you to leave the church or disaffiliate?" can be a good way to get started.

I'd also suggest looking for events that match the spiritual temperature of your friends and inviting them in. These might include one-off concerts, films, speakers and service opportunities that enable moderns to dip their toe back in the living water, or ongoing care gatherings such as Alcoholics Anonymous or divorce support groups that meet in churches or at least have a spiritual angle. Also consider passing around books that tell stories of redemption in the lives of Christian athletes and celebrities, and see what God might do.

Bruce, mentioned in the conversation above, is ten years my senior. Here's a dialogue with a modern college student.

"Sarita, you've decided not to be involved in a church. What led you to that decision?"

"I went to church to please my parents. It was a family thing. Now they're not around."

"Were you getting anything out of your home church?"

"Yeah, the people. It was a good community. But in college I have my own friends, and they don't go to church. It's cool."

"How about the beliefs you learned at your church?"

"Oh, I still believe in God. And I pray. But I don't think you need to go to church or be involved in the institution to be spiritual. Studies have shown that religion is probably just one of our instincts that developed through evolution. Besides, there's lots of other religions out there. I don't think you have to stick to just one thing."

That exchange is typical of many conversations I've had with students in my travels. Notice the important words: "parents," "community," "God," "prayer," "science," "other religions." So many places to pursue conversation. With Sarita in Chicago, I went for the evolution topic. Just because science has an explanation for human beings' religious impulse doesn't make religion false. Besides, Sarita believes in God anyway, albeit defined rather vaguely.

My next step (had I had more time with Sarita, which I didn't) would have been to examine the claims of Christ and the authority he brings from God to reveal truth. Right down Broadway for a modernist, assuming she's interested. Eventually, you want to invite people to read the accounts of Jesus' life with you, maybe in a four-week study of the Gospels. In InterVarsity we call them GIGs—Groups Investigating God. In this setting you let the Scriptures themselves speak powerfully to the mind and heart of a seeking person.

CHAPTER SUMMARY

Point to truth. Moderns tend to believe there is one truth about the world, which can be discovered and discussed rationally. Moderns are less likely than postmoderns, for example, to say, "That's true for you but not for me." So try to lead modern folks to the one who said, "I am the way and the truth and the life" (John 14:6).

Point to heaven and hell. Many moderns maintain a God conscience, whether clear or vague in their minds. Older moderns are often caught up in a works righteousness that attempts to earn God's favor. Grace can seem a foreign concept, but grace is, of course, the real anecdote. Try to build your communication around Ephesians 2:8. Learn it, paraphrase it, communicate it with your own grace.

Prepare for the unbelief of believers. Many moderns are skeptics and believers at the same time: skeptical of religion due to the power of science and the failures of religious institutions, but believers in an overarching deity to answer big questions and provide moral guidance. Many are dropouts from organized religion. Asking gently about this disaffiliation can be a good place to start.

We've only scratched the surface when it comes to reaching out to moderns who are still theists of some variety. Nevertheless, time to move on to the atheists.

16

HOW TO TALK WITH MODERN ATHEISTS

ATHEISTS TEND TO BE MY CROWD. Ever since my conversion in 1976, God has given me so many friendships with atheists that I cannot remember them all. Some have become Christians, though not many. Some enter my life by the front door, stay for a year or two, and exit out the back. I don't know what happened to them.

On college campuses I gravitate toward secular student alliances and freethinkers clubs. Some are friendly and respectful, others not so much. Sometimes I'm invited as the guest interview for their weekly meetings. I do get nervous on most occasions, wondering if I'll be able to come up with concise replies to aggressive lines of questioning, which sometimes I can't. Even so, I'm slowly learning the value of being present to atheists, of trusting God and showing his love, of offering the best defense of the faith that I can in the moment, and leaving the results to the Lord.

What follows, then, are nine suggestions for relating to modern-thinking atheists, born of a thousand conversations. Then I'll share some common practices atheists use in their interactions with Christians, to help prepare you for engagement.

REACHING MODERN ATHEISTS

Here are some important things to keep in mind as you interact with atheists.

Care. Your decision, made in advance, to care for an atheist friend will carry you a long way. Nothing can substitute for genuine compassion, encouragement and generosity. Sometimes this is tough because atheists can be abrasive and off-putting (as can Christians, unfortunately). Nevertheless, we Christians are the ones with the power of the Holy Spirit, and we're the ones armed with the command to love our neighbors—and our enemies.

Sad to say, Christians sometimes forget this command when it matters most—in the middle of a dialogue, allowing anger to take over their good intent. You'll also find that caregiving acts like oil in a relationship, preventing friendly debate from deteriorating over the long haul into competition.

Pray. Inevitably as you get to know an atheist in deeper ways, you'll encounter specific barriers to faith—probably many. You'd think these barriers would be mostly intellectual, but that may not be the case. Often atheists believe in God from a young age, but at some point they experience something negative with religion that pushes them the other way. In atheism, they find intellectual reasons to support their distaste for Christians or Muslims or the whole enterprise of faith.

Praying your way into these underlying motivations can be very helpful. Just be ready to encounter the kind of hardness of heart that makes Pharaoh look like a softy. Then you'll really need to pray, because hardheartedness isn't overcome through argumentation. Recall Paul's warning against intellectualism in 1 Corinthians 1–2 and his appeal to a "demonstration of the Spirit's power" (1 Corinthians 2:4). Let us tap into this power through prayer.

Play your whole orchestra. See chapter two on this topic and the value of making a cumulative case for faith. The point is to bring breadth to your relationships with atheists—that is, wholeness. In other words, develop into a person who reads widely, thinks broadly, and pursues the arts, literature and culture. Know something about politics, travel and relationships. Integrate faith into everything. Play all the instruments in your orchestra. A couple of times I've taken non-Christian friends to art galleries to discuss paintings—a fun outing that comes with the added benefit of unlocking some of their opinions and basic beliefs.

After I've hung out for a while with atheists in my travels and at home, they sometimes say, "You're not like other Christians." That is, they don't see me as anti-intellectual and narrow. They're surprised that I read outside my own tradition, that I support science and don't take the Bible on blind faith. Ironically, some atheists are pretty narrow themselves, focusing tightly on science, personal gratification and fighting religion. So when I demonstrate breadth in my life, it's prophetic—a soft critique of their world. But of course I must not think of this difference as triumphalism or one-upmanship; I simply wish to be a broad person naturally. Created in the image of God, I find myself interested in all of God's vast world. So when I bring a measure of breadth to a relationship with an atheist, I'm just being myself.

Use your head. Remember that atheists are usually committed to finding certainty and objective truth. Many have thought deeply about the world and worked out their beliefs, so you must try to engage their intellect. That's where they live! If you enter the relationship with prayerful caring and thinking, you'll enjoy many great conversations and friendships. But if you align yourself with the anti-intellectualism often found in evangelical circles, you'll be playing right into the hands (and Christian stereotypes) of atheists.[1] If the intellectual approach to things just isn't your strong point, it's okay. Try to provide your atheist friends with helpful resources such as books and other Christians who are gifted in this area.

Distinguish between the "new" atheists and all the rest. The new atheism is led by four identifiable figures: Richard Dawkins, Sam

Harris, Daniel Dennett and the late Christopher Hitchens. Dawkins is probably most well-known. The new atheism is characterized by its combative posture and has often been described as fundamentalist in nature. Alister McGrath comments, "Dawkins simply offers the atheist equivalent of slick hellfire preaching, substituting turbocharged rhetoric and highly selective manipulation of facts for careful, evidence-based thinking."[2]

Alvin Plantinga calls this new breed of atheists vastly inferior to the "old" atheists, such as Bertrand Russell and John Mackie, as well as contemporary thinkers such as William Rowe and Thomas Nagel. Plantinga adds, "We may perhaps hope that the new atheists are but a temporary blemish on the face of serious conversation in this crucial area."[3]

One reason for singling out the new atheists is that their devotees are growing, especially among young people. Their underlying frustrations at feeling oppressed by religion have been given voice, like a match struck to dry tinder, by Dawkins and company. And they've quickly adopted the mocking, dissing style of their mentors. One night at a campus in Minnesota, my talk was disrupted by a strident atheist who accused me of telling lies to my audience. He continued to badger and interrupt until organizers threatened to kick him out. I remember how bold he was, so certain of his beliefs and so disinterested in anything contrary. At another campus, atheists clustered in the front rows during my presentation and threw out sarcastic questions and objections amidst much snickering. Disappointing but not surprising.

Deconstruct. Don't be afraid to change positions in the debate. Usually atheists are the ones making accusations against Christians, and we're defending ourselves. Try it the other way round by deconstructing the other side.[4] Begin by asking atheists how they find ethical guidance and meaning for their lives in a meaningless universe. One thing to avoid, however, is accusing atheists of not having any meaning or morality in their lives. Of course they do! But we rightly ask for a basis for these things in a purely material world.

Ask about the effects of atheistic indoctrination of kids and families in twentieth-century Soviet Union. Ask about the origin of the universe, the big bang, all kinds of topics. Ask the atheist to defend philosophical naturalism. Ask about evolution. Ask how she can trust her mind, evolved from monkeys, to be giving her accurate knowledge of the world. Ask whether human beings have any true free will in a physical universe. Ask what love is. Again, don't accuse. Don't wag your finger. Don't stoop to manipulation or sarcasm. Just ask and listen. If you find a hole, poke at it. Enjoy your friend, and hopefully you'll learn something that will challenge your faith and make you think.[5]

Another excellent question is to ask whether providing good evidence for Christ would actually make any difference. I like to use this question after a lot of water has flowed under the bridge, after I've made my case over a period of weeks or months. If you use the question too soon, it shuts down conversation on a negative response. It seems to me that an atheist doesn't always know what he would find ultimately convincing. If he thinks nothing could ever persuade him of God's existence and love, he could be wrong about that. Give it some time. People don't know themselves as well as Jesus knows them.

Retreat when necessary. Sometimes you hit a stalemate with atheists, and then it's time to retreat and pray. In more technical language, when epistemic common ground is lost, it's time to retreat to a tribal perspective and speak from within your narrative. That means you no longer assume that you and the atheist are judging the universe from the same platform. In fact, the platform is gone. You're simply talking past each other. Just admit that, and begin prefacing every statement, either verbally or as an implication, with, "From a Christian perspective . . . ," or, "The Bible teaches . . ." Now all you're doing is teaching your skeptical friend what Christians believe and trusting the Holy Spirit. It's no longer a "direct" exchange, back and forth, on each point. You're not on a journey together anymore. Rather, you're just two neighboring worldviews ("tribes") sharing information with each other. You're saying, "This is how things seem to me."[6]

But hey, it's okay. Over the course of your conversations, hopefully you've provided your friend with a rich and attractive alternative to an empty universe. If at some point she refuses to engage with you anymore, you've lost her. At least for now. But of course you can only do your part as you trust the Holy Spirit. You can't do her part. She's responsible for her faith, not you. I can tell you from experience that these relationships and conversations can be exhausting, so sometimes I'm reduced to saying to the Lord, "I'm feeling powerless. God, she's in your hands. I'm just the messenger here." In fact, I should probably be confessing that sentiment all the time.

Find the passive-active balance. Let me be very candid and tell you that it's not easy working with atheists. Often they're all over the map: a thousand unsupported assertions, accusations and generalizations. They may use rhetoric more than argumentation, though that's not always true. Some are sharp, caring and focused— just my kind of person. But quite often they've done little more than read a Dawkins book, watched an online debate or two and visited a few atheist websites. Then they come at you hard like you're stupid and know nothing. So be patient. That's just how it is.

Here's the key: Speak but don't trust in your speaking. What do I mean? I'm saying that if you want to really trust God and not your own apologetic efforts for your friend's salvation, then keep doing apologetics. That's the biblical tension. If you trust God but don't speak, you're too passive. If you speak but don't trust God, you're too active and your words will be impotent. Do both. Study, learn, bone up, strategize, hone your skills, go to training, develop a plan, talk, witness, strive, love, argue. And trust in none of this. Give it all to the Lord. Again, you're just the messenger. A good representative passage for this passive-active balance is found in Philippians 3:3, where Paul says we "serve God by his Spirit" and put "no confidence in the flesh." Then in Philippians 3:12-13 Paul talks about "pressing" and "straining" toward his goal. You and I should do the same.

Remember the power of community. Did you know you're not alone in witness? One of my main goals in evangelism is to get seekers and skeptics involved in my church and campus fellowship. There they can see the power of Christ worked out on an everyday basis. They get sustained exposure to Jesus as he is manifested in his people. They encounter people different from me who bring fresh voices and perspectives to the table. And hopefully they feel the supernatural love of the Spirit in our midst. In fact, I'd go so far as to say that Christian community is the number one apologetic for the truth of Christianity.

ATHEIST TACTICS

There's a common set of tactics that atheists—especially the "new" atheists—use. If you're aware of them in advance, your conversations will be more productive and your witness more effective. Here's a sampling:

Throwing sand in the air. Atheists like to barrage you with a hundred objections all at once. Thus I've gotten into the habit of asking which "grain of sand" they want me to address, because I can't respond to every particle in a cloud of dust.

Getting off topic. It's rare for an atheist to go all the way to the bottom of any topic. Usually when I drill down pretty far on a single topic, they jump ship and return to attack mode on something else. We need to ask them to stay on topic.

Using ridicule as a form of argumentation. You'd think atheists, of all people, supposedly committed to rational processes, would be the last to resort to sarcasm, putdowns and ridicule to make their points. Alas, not so. At least not these days. One evening at a large campus in the Midwest, our group held a friendly debate

with the local atheist club—except for the "friendly" part. They
mocked our team all evening. But I was proud of the Christian
students who served as panelists. Their posture of respect and
"turning the other cheek" was, I believe, a meaningful statement to
the audience. I remember one of the teenage atheists rolling his
eyes and laughing at my remarks several times. I can tell you with
absolute certainty that I've read more atheist philosophy than he
has. But so be it. The call and empowering of Jesus is to love our
enemies and not strike back.

Reading the Bible flat. By "flat" I mean thinking of all parts of the
Bible as being equally relevant for today. Thus it is common for
atheists to pick out the most arcane sections of the Old Testament,
state that "it's in the Bible," then shoot it down along with the
whole Bible. An example would be the prohibition against com-
bining two kinds of fabric in one's clothing (Leviticus 19:19). But
for the Christian, the coming of the Messiah and the writing of the
New Testament changes everything. The story of salvation has been
updated. Atheists are often unaware of the implications of this up-
dating, however, so it is our job to bring it to light. Ironically,
atheists tend to be literalists when it comes to reading the Bible, and
as mentioned earlier, they have trouble staying on topic. Let me
tease this out a bit:

ATHEIST: It says in Leviticus 20:10 to stone two people who
             commit adultery together. But in the New Tes-
             tament Jesus lets a woman off the hook who's been
             caught in adultery. See, the Bible contradicts itself.

CHRISTIAN: Leviticus was just the beginning of God shaping
             his people into a holy nation. Many of those laws
             are no longer in effect now that Jesus has come.

ATHEIST: But the Word of God can't be changed. It stands
             forever.

CHRISTIAN: You're right. But the Word of God is not just a rule book; it's a story book. It's the story of salvation. Here's an analogy: I treat my kids differently now than when they were in grade school. I haven't changed. My standards haven't changed. But they've changed. They're in a new chapter of life, and the old rules about things like avoiding busy streets no longer apply. The story has been updated.

ATHEIST: You're just embarrassed by all the stupid things in the Bible. You're trying to be evasive.

CHRISTIAN: We're talking about questions of theology and hermeneutics—the art of Bible interpretation—here. Have you ever studied these disciplines?

ATHEIST: I don't have to. Christians are literalists but they're not taking the Bible literally like they claim. God's Word doesn't change, because God doesn't change. But you're saying he does change. You're contradicting yourself; you're trapped and you know it.

CHRISTIAN: I ask you again, have you ever studied theology—meaning, the relation of the big themes of the Bible to each other?

ATHEIST: Sounds like a study about nothing. Your God is a sadistic murderer. I would never believe in a god like that.

CHRISTIAN: Wait, I thought we were talking about how to interpret the Bible. You seem to have changed the subject.

ATHEIST: You have absolutely no proof that the Christian God exists. I don't believe in God for the same reason I

> don't believe in unicorns. There's not a shred of evi-
> dence that the Bible is true. It's all just stupid legends
> and myths, designed to control people.

At this point a bunch of skeptics in the room are nodding their
heads with approval, as if the atheist just made a great argument
against the ignorant Christian.

> CHRISTIAN: Now you're starting to throw sand in the air. Which
> grain of sand do you want me to respond to?

> ATHEIST: You just take all this religion crap on blind faith
> and then you impose it on everyone else. There's
> no way I'd ever be a superstitious idiot Christian.
> The Bible has been used to justify slavery and the
> oppression of women. . . . And I suppose you've
> never heard of the Crusades?

And so it goes. I've had various versions of that conversation
dozens of times. At some point you have to call the person on their
topic hopping and try to get down to the real issue: in this case,
Bible interpretation. Sometimes I say this: "You seem to think it's
easy to interpret the Bible. I actually find it difficult, which is quite
ironic. I'm interested in knowing what the original biblical authors
intended, and I want to learn from professional commentators. Are
you willing to take that approach as well? Then maybe we could
have a productive discussion about this."

Unfortunately, many atheists are interested only in their own
naive reading of the text and won't pursue a deeper exchange of
ideas with me. The good news is that our faithfulness in hanging
in there on these conversations sometimes leads to collateral fruit.
A more thoughtful skeptic sitting on the sidelines may approach
you after hearing your dialogue, and this is the person you are
meant to talk with. This is the person God has touched, and the
Holy Spirit has used a lesser conversation to launch a better one.

Apologist James Sire once said to me that it's not always the truth that's heard that makes a difference; it's the truth that's *overheard*. I encourage you to keep having conversations. Keep at it. Find your voice, show care and respect to your dialogue partners, and at some point you'll end up bumping into the person God is drawing to himself. Then you'll see the fruit of your labors.

Invoking the good name of science against you. Atheists like to talk about a "scientific" worldview that's committed to logic and facts. Any statement, such as "God exists," that doesn't measure up to the standards of scientific verification doesn't count as meaningful at all and is really a statement about nothing. The only way it can be believed, so says the atheist, is on blind faith, since there is no direct evidence visible to the senses to support it.

The most obvious response here is that no part of this discussion is scientific at all. In other words, atheist claims such as "All statements must be scientifically verifiable to be meaningful" turn out to be self-refuting, for the claim itself is not scientifically verifiable. You couldn't put that claim under a microscope or test it empirically or make it visible to the senses. See chapter twelve and the bricklayer analogy for further analysis.[7]

LEE

Currently I'm in a stalemate with my atheist friend Lee in a ten-year dialogue that takes place mostly on email, occasionally in person. Our most common topic is the historical reliability (or lack thereof) of the New Testament. But we seem to have differing standards regarding what counts as reliable. Standards such as verifiability, precision, multiple witnesses and so forth are defined and weighted using the tools of philosophy, but Lee rejects almost all philosophy— even that of atheists. Hence our stalemate. I love the guy. I pray for him. But I'm not sure how to get out of our current predicament. Just being real with you here.

TOM

Unfortunately, Christians often think atheists are hopeless cases. Some believers are quick to invoke the well-known verse "Do not throw your pearls to pigs" (Matthew 7:6). I'm not against this verse. It's in the Bible. But it ought to be a last resort after everything else has failed. In fact, atheists do sometimes come to faith. I led a seminar at an Urbana Mission Convention where I described some characteristics of the new atheists. A student approached me afterward and said, "That was me. Exactly me. I was blind but somehow God had mercy on me." I'm glad the Christian witness in his life didn't give up on him.

My friend Tom was in the same boat. He'd grown up in the church but had many doubts about how God interacted with the world, and why suffering and evil are so prevalent. He went off to Notre Dame and studied philosophy, where he found himself embroiled in the classical arguments for God's existence. By the time he left college for law school at the University of Minnesota, he was agnostic in his outlook, perhaps leaning toward atheism. He didn't think anyone was in good position to judge whether God is real or merely a myth.

Tom stayed in touch with the arguments on both sides of the equation. Subjective claims of experiencing God by believers were in theory subject to scientific critique. But he wondered if science was actually the right tool for the job. As for himself, he had no mystical experiences that could be attributed to God. Every claim of spiritual connections to God were from other people. He and I talked on occasion and I offered the occasional apologetic resource. He came to Hamline University in St. Paul with me one evening and listened to a debate on God's existence. At the close of the event he engaged the Christian debater, Professor David Clark, for about twenty minutes one on one. It was intense. Yet there was no subsequent change that I could tell in Tom's beliefs. I kept praying.

Tom's breakthrough came from two unexpected sources: history and church. As an attorney he had a sense for the credibility of historical claims, and when he began to read Lee Strobel and N. T. Wright, the figure of Jesus as a true historical figure who performed miracles and rose from the dead began to make sense.[8]

The second breakthrough came at a Lutheran Church he'd been attending as a nonbeliever with his wife, Kathe. Her own renewal of faith and personal vitality was a definite influence on Tom, but somehow the whole issue of Christian faith was crystallized by a large painting of Jesus mounted in a hallway at the church. The caption read, "Who do you say that I am?" Every time Tom walked past that painting he was reminded that he needed to answer the question for himself, because it was the ultimate question of the universe.

I visited Tom's law office one day and asked him how the spiritual journey was going. His answer startled me. "I've been praying during my drive to work every day."

What?

"I've come to believe the historical evidence for the life of Jesus," he continued. "Rick, Christianity is true."

You're kidding. I was shocked, though I tried not to show it. The skeptic had turned to faith. This all took place a few years ago, and Tom will tell you to this day that he still has doubts and that he thinks about the great questions regularly.

Recently I visited Tom in the new office that houses his law firm. We enjoyed an hour of sharing and fellowship and closed our time in prayer. He and Kathe have begun hosting InterVarsity retreats at their lake home where they share their amazing testimony of faith with college students.

SUGGESTED RESOURCES

J. P. Moreland and Kai Nielsen, *Does God Exist? The Great Debate* (Nashville: Thomas Nelson, 1990).

David K. Clark, *Dialogical Apologetics* (Grand Rapids, MI: Baker, 1993).

Antony Flew and Roy Abraham Varghese, *There Is a God: How the World's Most Notorious Atheist Changed His Mind* (New York: HarperOne, 2007).

Alister McGrath and Joanna Collicutt McGrath, *The Dawkins Delusion? Atheist Fundamentalism and the Denial of the Divine* (Downers Grove, IL: IVP Books, 2007).

17

HOW TO TALK WITH POSTMODERN SEEKERS AND SKEPTICS

WHEN I LOOK BACK ON all the conversations with skeptics that I've had over the years, I'd have to sincerely rate myself with mostly Bs and Cs, an occasional D and the rare A. Just being gut-honest.

Here was a D: As was the case with many of my non-Christian friends and acquaintances, I met Gordon on the golf course through some mutual friends. Think of your favorite social activity or sport, and you'll know exactly how comfortable I am in the environs of golf: the manicured grasses, the competition of the game, the repartee with my pals. It's totally me.

Gordon's Lexus SUV was cool and soft as I climbed in, and we'd no more than wheeled out of the parking lot when he launched into the topic of religion. He began by filling me in on his spiritual background, which involved experimenting with a variety of spiritualities. Then he asked a question: "How do you know you've chosen the right religion?"

I was giddy. Eighty-one and sunny in St. Paul that afternoon, the golf had been spectacular, and now dream day was closing off with a chat about my favorite subject matter—God. In a luxury ride. Feeling the moment, I dove headlong into the topic of religious pluralism and explained to Gordon that not all religions can be true because they tend to contradict each other, and then I spelled out a couple of those contradictions.

My response hit Gordon like a ton of nothing. He kept talking about his experiences with meditation and his desire to find fulfillment and spiritual grounding. Wasn't he listening to me? I countered with something about the historical Jesus and how we could know that he really was the Son of God. . . .

Disconnect. Gordon and I were on different planes. I might as well have been talking about the color of eighty-three.

Unfortunately, in this conversation I'd skipped a crucial step—listening. I hadn't bothered. Oh, I'd made a show of it. I'd remained quiet while Gordon talked, but my listening had been passive because I was actually busy with something else: planning my response. Gordon shared his life while I nodded and smiled and ignored him. Bad move on my part.

I wish I'd have engaged in active listening, what Rick Richardson calls "detective work" in evangelism.[1] In evangelism a good detective adopts a learning posture. She essentially says to the other person, "Teach me about you. I'm all ears." Had I really listened to Gordon, I'd have discovered that he was moving along a postmodern path, while I had missed a turn somewhere and was wandering around in modern land. So here we were, same vehicle, seated a foot apart—in different worlds. No wonder we couldn't communicate.

FIVE THRESHOLDS OF CONVERSION

So how do we relate to postmodern non-Christians? What are the keys? Had I been more open to who the real Gordon was, I'd have thought about the five thresholds of postmodern conversion laid out so beautifully by Everts and Shaupp.[2] After analyzing hundreds of stories of students coming to faith in Southern California over a ten-year period, they noticed patterns recurring in the accounts.

They simply wrote down these patterns in *I Once Was Lost*—a must-read for anyone serious about outreach to postmoderns.

Here are the five thresholds, with my own commentary inserted. The authors stress that not everyone who comes to faith follows this exact script, and sometimes people move back and forth between stages. Nevertheless, the overall pattern holds true.

First threshold: from distrust to trust. This stage has a lot to do with trusting a Christian, so it's often very relational. It can take a long time for postmodern skeptics to come to faith, because many have a built-in distrust of the institution of Christianity. So they're starting in spiritual deficit. Postmoderns are sensitive to issues of power and oppression. Thus the perceived marginalizing of women, minorities and gays in the history of the church is off-putting to them.

In coming to trust a Christian, however, their stereotypes of the church can be gradually dismantled. I once spent a weekend in the company of a distant relative who was openly gay as part of a family reunion. He knew I was an evangelical Christian and was quite leery of me at first. We seemed to hit it off all weekend, however, which surprised him, he said afterward. That's it, isn't it? I want to be surprising in the ways that Jesus was (and is). More on that below.

Second threshold: from complacent to curious. Just because a person begins to trust a Christian doesn't mean he is necessarily interested in Christianity. Everts and Schaupp warn Christians several times not to skip ahead in witness, past where the Holy Spirit has brought a skeptical person. This is great advice. Many non-Christians feel satisfied with their lives, and even if they aren't, they don't necessarily think of Christ as a possible solution.

Quite honestly, complacency and indifference are significant barriers to faith. Just getting someone interested in spiritual things is sometimes a big job. It requires prayer, patience and strategic thinking. Rick Richardson suggests "soul-awakening" events, where people's natural hunger for God is evoked and brought to the surface. For the complacent person, then, think about their felt needs, such as community, fun, acceptance, meaning and romance. And think of ways to connect those needs to the gospel—by bringing people into Christian community, inviting them to service opportunities, engaging their questions and opinions through movies and cultural events that raise big issues.[3]

At my church, we are treated often to video testimonies of folks in our congregation who've taken significant steps of faith, perhaps toward baptism. These stories are so compelling and so effective at evoking spiritual hunger that they tend to come in waves. One story sparks other stories, which spark others, and so on. Complacency is challenged, curiosity is piqued, spiritual hunger is aroused and people awaken from slumber to the possibilities of faith.

Also, I'll mention the ministry of prophetic prayer and power encounters. I wish I could say I am experienced and expert at this ministry, but that's not the case. I've seen it in action up close and heard many cool stories but only dabbled in it myself. In my city of St. Paul, Christian teams sometimes go out and pray for people in the streets and parks, often sharing special words of knowledge or images that come to mind in prayer, then asking if these items "connect" for the person—which they frequently do. Some of these images are concrete, such as a shovel or dance shoes or a house in the woods; others are more abstract, such as encouragement for loneliness or sickness. Recipients often say, "How did you know that about me?"

These encounters with the Holy Spirit can touch the heart of a complacent postmodern, whether she was the person prayed for or was someone who observed the encounter or heard the reports later. The apostle Paul wrote, "My message and my preaching were not with wise and persuasive words, but with a demonstration of the Spirit's power, so that your faith might not rest on human wisdom, but on God's power" (1 Corinthians 2:4-5). As evangelicals gradually recover the ministry of prayer, prophecy and healing, secular postmoderns could be in for a significant blessing—and awakening.

Third threshold: from closed to open to change. Everts and Schaupp again warn that our non-Christian friend is not yet a "seeker," not yet directly interested in pursuing life change. Altar calls and harvest events are not necessarily appropriate during the first three stages, though in some cases such calls can plant the seed for future faith decisions. For the present, however, the person needs to consider the possibility of a major life revision, which can seem very daunting. Sometimes I imagine myself walking into a mosque or Mormon temple and ask what it would take to convert from evangelical Christianity to a different faith. Nearly impossible for me, I'd say. That's how postmodern skeptics sometimes feel. What seems to us a natural progression toward Christ can look quite different from their standpoint.

Yet change happens. Closed hearts open. How? Everts and Schaupp share their secret: we have no idea. It's a mystery. They cite the parable of the man who scatters seed, which sprouts and grows day and night, though the man doesn't know how. "All by itself the soil produces grain—first the stalk, then the head, then the full kernel in the head. As soon as the grain is ripe, he puts the sickle to it, because the harvest has come" (Mark 4:26-29).

We're talking the basics here, nothing very fancy: prayer, care, Scripture. After establishing trust and emerging from complacency in the first two stages, perhaps the postmodern friend is open to studying the accounts of Jesus for himself, with you as a guide, and gradually opening himself to life change. That's what happened to Justin Weber at the University of Wisconsin Eau Claire. As a first-year student, he came to campus thoroughly established in the party scene and nursing a bad drinking problem. Christians befriended him, opened up to him—and he to them.

Next thing was a GIG (short for Groups Investigating God, an evangelistic Bible study), studying Jesus for himself, eventually opening his heart to change and coming to faith. The posture of "change" in his heart resulted from the quality of life he saw in

Christians—not their perfection; he never expected that. Rather, he was influenced by their authenticity, faith, perseverance, strength. He knew he needed those qualities for himself and that he would never find his true self inside the cage of alcohol and sex. Today, Justin leads fruitful, faith-producing GIGs for other students.

Fourth threshold: from meandering to seeking. Finally, a true seeker! For many skeptics, it's been a long journey. Though sometimes God speeds along the faith journey from zero to sixty in short order, mostly it's an extended process of distrusting, resisting, searching, doubting, wavering and then finally actively pursuing God. Amy was a student who came from a church background that was decidedly not evangelical. Somehow getting involved in Inter-Varsity in college, she felt out of place at times. Whenever I came through town, we'd meet up. I said to her that I thought Inter-Varsity would always be an "eighty percenter" for her—that there would be twenty percent of what we do and who we are that she'd struggle with, especially evangelism.

Amy agreed. Thing is, she was already working on one of her friends who'd been recalcitrant toward God and the church. This was a disconnect for me—the non-evangelist doing evangelism. Amy prayed for her friend, invited her to Bible studies and other meetings. No response. Then, for whatever reason, her friend finally accepted the invitation to come to a spring conference. I was the speaker. I remember giving the call to faith, stretching it out a bit and catching Amy's hopeful eye. Finally, on the "last call," her friend came forward and was immediately engulfed in a mass bear hug by all the students from her school. Amy cried. Her friend the wanderer had become a seeker, then had become a Christian. What an arduous journey! And what a fine travel guide the non-evangelist had been.

But I guess I'm getting ahead of myself. Crossing into the kingdom is the next threshold.

Fifth threshold: from seeking to crossing into the kingdom. When postmodernism hit campuses hard in the nineties, I began meeting with Erik at Macalester College. Talk about a cool guy—he was outgoing, bright and an excellent musician who ran several bands during his college days. At the invitation of a student named Andrew, he'd joined a GIG during spring semester of his freshman year, so he was up and running on the path toward faith. At the time I was scrambling to adjust to the postmodern mindset. I remember sitting in the union studying the Gospels and talking music, world-views and literature with Erik in his sophomore year. Though I didn't know about the five thresholds then, I was fortunate enough to enter his life when he was opening to the possibility of change (third stage), then crossing to the seeker threshold. Erik continued his journey. We kept talking. Without much church background, the evangelical world of our ministry at Macalester felt like a cross-cultural experience for him.

"I was ten years behind other students in reading the Bible," he recalled recently. Yet they welcomed him, loved him, gently challenged him to move forward. He studied abroad at St. Andrews his junior year, where he met more Christians who encouraged his budding faith. Somewhere in the whole process he crossed a line. He went from not a full follower of Jesus to true followership. Actually, his conversion was gradual and nonchalant, perfectly postmodern, and he remains so to this day: a high school English teacher, poet, songwriter, social activist and successful musician around the Midwest.[4] He continues to deal with the angst—and wonder, he would tell you—of being an artistic, three-dimensional Jesus devotee in an evangelical subculture that from his perspective is often characterized by black-and-white thinking and false certitude about spiritual matters.

The secret to Erik's conversion? Envision me shrugging my shoulders right now. In the external world there were Bible studies with Andrew, myself and others. There were Christian friendships and retreats. We prayed for him. The seed was planted. It sprouted and grew—but exactly how? Beats me.

POSTMODERN APOLOGETICS

It's difficult to recommend a specific conversational approach for postmodern outreach, because in real life postmoderns come in many shades of gray. Of several important issues that could be addressed, I will choose two common ones—truth and tolerance.[5]

Truth. Darren is a socially minded activist who uses his belief in God to motivate his concern for the poor and marginalized in society. This I applaud. One day I asked his permission to present him with an intellectual challenge. He agreed. It went like this:

"Darren, generally speaking you stand in the Christian tradition, and you care about justice and mercy in society."

"Yes."

"You also believe that your Christian tradition is no more true, necessarily, than any other tradition—that in fact there are many truths, none of which are privileged over any other. Is that right?"

"Yes."

"But isn't that a form of relativism—meaning truth is relative to the perspective of the person holding it?"

"I guess you could say that. I'm not sure I want to be labeled a relativist, but right now I can't think of a way around it. Maybe I am a relativist."

"It seems to me that relativists are saying, implicitly, that relativism is true. How do you respond to that?"

"That puts me in an uncomfortable position."

Indeed. Relativism is self-refuting. It makes the truth claim that there is no truth. To be fair, the underlying motive of many relativists—to show respect and to refrain from the "power play" of imposing one's view on others—is commendable. But to say that your relativism is "true" is intellectually inconsistent.[6]

Tolerance. The same strategy can be used for the issue of tolerance. Secular postmoderns are known for recommending the virtue of tolerance and practicing it by tolerating a diversity of viewpoints. But every time there is an exception to the rule, tolerance becomes intolerant. For example, if a person believes in tolerance but fails to tolerate Muslims or evangelical Christians or certain political viewpoints, she has become intolerant. Or selectively tolerant. True tolerance, it seems to me, respects all people as God's image bearers and seeks common ground when available while disagreeing when necessary.

The type of critique of truth and tolerance I just made can feel jarring along the path of conversion for postmodern people. Stylistically, it seems out of place in their universe. The best I can say is, use with caution. Notice that with Darren I asked his permission to challenge his thinking. That's because I knew I was about to undermine his world if he took my critique seriously, which he did. Thus we need to stay on top of our "detective work," listening closely to God regarding when—and if—it's appropriate to bring philosophical argumentation against postmodernism.

A brick in a pillowcase. In chapter fourteen I suggested a representative image for modernism—a brick, due to its firmness and sturdy foundations—and postmodernism—a pillow, due to its softer feel and less-defined boundaries. One of the most common profiles of students I meet on college campuses is what I'm calling a brick in a pillowcase. These folks are pillow on the surface and brick underneath, meaning they are stylistically but not substantively postmodern. They project an outer layer of postmodern traits, such as being oriented to story, power relations and community. But at their core they are rational in a more modern way. They think of the world as one single reality about which persons of diverse perspectives can talk.

Thus it takes postmodern invitations to first begin to engage with them: relational trust-building, stories and the arts, concern for service and justice. But then at some point they want to think through the issues logically. They want answers and are not as comfortable with ambiguity and dissonance as true postmoderns. So if we are going to follow Paul's calling to "become all things to all people" (1 Corinthians 9:22), we'll need first to wear the hat of postmodern connectivity, then later put on the hat of modernist, rational case making.

Telling stories. Postmodernism is known for its love of story in at least two ways. In epistemology, which is the study of knowledge and how we know, story has taken the place of objective truth. Thus for postmoderns every group and community has its own story or narrative, and the world is made up of each group contributing its own story to the whole rather than by all the groups subscribing to one grand story or truth (such as Christianity or atheism or Islam).

Secondly, postmoderns tend to love great stories. At Macalester, the popular radio personality Garrison Keillor, whose weekly show "A Prairie Home Companion" airs from St. Paul, occasionally appears on campus to read poetry and tell stories, and his crowds are standing room only. In other venues at the college, the chaplain sponsors a series of gatherings called "Sacred Stories" for students who want to hear the spiritual journeys of other students and share their own, and on a certain evening in December, students come to the chapel in their PJs to listen to faculty and staff read holiday stories.

All this to say that one of the best ways to reach postmoderns is to tell stories. I'm just learning the art of storytelling myself, and I recommend two fine books on the subject: *Experiential Storytelling* and *Telling the Gospel Through Story*.[7] The first is written in a youth ministry context and talks about creating settings of experiential learning for students. The second book is about the art of storytelling itself and includes resources and training for telling God's story in a series of smaller stories. Really impressive stuff, and I plan to work on this art form in order to increase my effectiveness in postmodern outreach. Join me?

Surprising, arresting Jesus stories. As a sidelight to my work in campus ministry, I have a small wedding business. It grew out of a need for couples getting married at my golf course to employ a chaplain for their ceremonies. As part of the required pre-marriage counseling, I ask couples to read the Gospel of John and answer three questions about Jesus: What's appealing? What's surprising? What do you learn about the various responses to him?

Most couples have a faint familiarity with Jesus from their background, but the reason they're getting married at a golf course is that they're not involved in a church. At least not currently. Few have read the Bible anytime in the recent past. Almost all find Jesus appealing, and the careful readers find him arresting. Few dislike him. It's the church they dislike, either as a matter of principle or because they grew bored with it.

This should be instructive to our outreach efforts with postmodern skeptics. Compared with their often stereotypical vision of the church, Jesus should come as a fresh breeze to their minds. One bride-to-be I worked with left the church angrily as a teenager and never went back. Yet in reading John's account, she came to see Jesus as a revolutionary against hypocrisy and big-business religion. "Rick, I actually like him," was her response. "Where was this Jesus when I was growing up in the church?"

The title of one of my campus outreach talks is "Wine, Woman and a Den of Thieves." It's a short exposé of three Jesus stories from John 2 and 4: the wedding at Cana, the cleansing of the temple, the woman at the well. In each case Jesus does the unexpected—things he "cannot" and "should not" do, according to common religious sensibilities. He provides alcohol to a party, he stands up to the religious establishment and he taints himself by contact with a certain lowly woman. These are the acts of a radical activist that would appeal to many postmodern folk—if we learn to tell the Jesus stories well and ask our friends to read them thoughtfully.[8]

Community. One of the foundational principles of postmodern thought (and living) is that community is the basis for everything else. Truth, power, friendship, politics, sexual identity, common interests, hobbies, work—it all flows from community. The ideal place for postmodern skeptics to discover Jesus is in Christian community. And this is where things can get dicey, because Christian community is often connected to the idea of church in the mind of a skeptic, and she may have prejudices against the church, whether historical (the Crusades and Inquisitions) or current (negative personal experiences or learned academic disdain). Despite the barriers, however, I'd strongly encourage you to pray, invite and persuade your friends into the flow of Christian community, the best apologetic for Christianity. Everts and Schaupp urge,

> Let your friends watch you do life together with your small group, and they will see forgiveness in action, reconciliation, people who speak the truth in love to each other, honoring one another with their words, healthy cross-gender relationships, care of the poor, the power of prayer. As you practice generosity and care for those in need in your church, bring your non-Christian friends with you. God's generosity is seen in your generous acts.[9]

Like the surprising, arresting Jesus, Christian community can serve as a point of intrigue for non-Christians. It can arouse curiosity. And it can feel like a potential new "connection" in the web of connectivity that makes up the postmodern world. Justin Weber, mentioned earlier, includes Christian community as a major component of his journey to faith. On a summer service project to Cancun, he met a translator who was a Christian student leader at the University of Wisconsin Eau Claire, and through this guy's hospitality, Justin found himself disassociating with the party scene and reestablishing his identity in the body of Christ—because he found the community so compelling.

THE CLOSING SCENE

Space considerations prevent me from writing much more about postmodern outreach, including the place of the arts, appealing to mystery, using hospitality, asking great questions, using service projects and road trips, and other related topics. Instead, I'll share a closing story that illustrates a few of these principles.

In 2013 I teamed up with a unique person to present a call to faith to three hundred college students gathered from several states, mostly Wisconsin, at a spring conference. The text assigned to me for the evening was Revelation 3, which includes, among other elements, two key references that could be employed for a postmodern altar call: the white robes of salvation (verses 5 and 18) and the book of life (verse 5).

Toward the end of my talk I described a modern-day man who was persecuted like many of the first-century Christians. Ahmed Haile served for many years as an agent of reconciliation between Muslim and Christian communities in East Africa. At one point in his dangerous career, his leg was blown off by a rocket grenade. Later he moved to Milwaukee with his family to fight a battle with cancer, which he lost in 2011.[10]

Then I introduced his daughter, Sofia, a student at Macalester. She made her way to the front, dressed in a white robe, as prescribed for the saints of Revelation 3. She performed a "slam poem"—a spoken word as tribute to her late father. It was performed with professional skill but also with the heart of a bereaved yet wildly hopeful daughter. The room was thunderstruck. I could not speak. I will never forget this sacred moment the rest of my life and beyond.

Finally I forced something out. Would students want to have that kind of hope in their lives? Would they want Sofia for their spiritual sister in Christ? Then come forward and declare your faith publicly. A line formed. Sofia greeted each student with a warm embrace, placed a white robe of salvation around their shoulders, guided them over to the book of life, got their names inked in the book, handed them a Bible and passed them off to an InterVarsity staff member for prayer.[11] Repeat for each student.

An hour and many tears later, it was over and we felt tired, elated and thankful. I hope you're able to glean some lessons for postmodern outreach from this story: the art of the poem, the story line of Sofia's father, the drama, the props, the connection of Scripture to real life, the beautiful setting. This was an ideal and unusual moment. But if we are in the mindset and habit of planting seeds of hospitality, story and meaningful dialogue for our postmodern friends, I believe God will do a great work. How, exactly? I have no idea.

EPILOGUE

A Word of Encouragement

IN THIS BOOK I HAVE TRIED to strike a balance between maximum preparation and maximum reliance on God's Spirit when it comes to conversations with seekers and skeptics. Perhaps the clearest statement of those two themes bound together is found in chapter sixteen under "Find the passive-active balance."

I find a shortage of both in my ministry. I get out there in front of a group of college students or church folk to make a case for Christian faith and I realize that I'm not as prepared as I should be. I hate that thought. It usually hits me about five minutes before I'm scheduled to start.

But I also feel the great temptation to be all about apologetic technique, where the danger, of course, is self-sufficiency. I take comfort in the words of veteran apologist James Sire:

> I suggest that one who seeks to defend the faith begin with the biblical testimony about Jesus. When objections arise . . . they can be shunted to the side for the moment. The point is

to get people to "look at" and, in a deeper sense, to "meet" Jesus in the Gospels. He is a compelling figure. . . . Conviction comes from an encounter with Jesus as prompted by the Holy Spirit. Abstract argument becomes academic when a person meets Jesus.[1]

Sire has also said many times in print and in my hearing that the best reason to believe in Christianity is Jesus.

That simplifies things considerably.

The images and illustrations found in these pages, if used well, will help simplify and organize your points in apologetic conversations. You'll be able to remember your lines a lot easier. You'll be quicker on the draw to say something meaningful and helpful rather than getting a sudden case of the "mutes" or the "ramblings" when it's your turn to speak up for God and the Bible.

But the real simplicity in these images will be found in the manner in which they point to Jesus. If you allow him to do his work through the seeds you are planting in others—through your words and manner—positive results will eventually come. And when fruit is born, you will be wise to just shrug your shoulders and admit, "I don't know how this really happened."

NOTES

CHAPTER 2: PLAY YOUR WHOLE ORCHESTRA

[1]This book is now in its fifth edition. James Sire, *The Universe Next Door: A Basic Worldview Catalog,* 5th ed. (Downers Grove, IL: IVP Academic, 2009).

[2]Douglas Groothuis, *Christian Apologetics: A Comprehensive Case for Biblical Faith* (Downers Grove, IL: IVP Academic, 2011), Kindle ed., chap. 9. In this particular instance Groothuis is actually referring to the cumulative case for theism in general, but the principle can be applied equally to Christianity, as he states in the same chapter: "The larger case for Christian theism includes even more lines of converging evidence, such as the resurrection of Christ."

[3]James K. Beilby, *Thinking About Christian Apologetics* (Downers Grove, IL: IVP Academic, 2011), p. 98.

[4]Groothuis argues for an incremental approach: "How does one present an argument for the Christian worldview as the best hypothesis? The answer: carefully, slowly and piece by piece." Groothuis, *Christian Apologetics,* chap. 3.

[5]Andy Crouch, *Culture Making: Recovering Our Creative Calling* (Downers Grove, IL: InterVarsity Press, 2008), p. 201.

[6]Had there been room for a response, I'd have said something about Adam and Eve fulfilling the mandate to "be fruitful and multiply," thus producing many children, including daughters, that Cain could have married. Yes, his wife would necessarily have been his sister (or niece), but the laws against marrying close relatives weren't given until the time of Moses.

[7]"God may use any means at his disposal, and all means are at his disposal." Groothuis, *Christian Apologetics*, chap. 3.

CHAPTER 3: HOW THE WORLD CAME TO BE

[1]The Pew Research Center reported in 2012 that twenty percent of US adults (thirty-five percent of adults under thirty) have no religious affiliation, including six percent who are atheist or agnostic. However, two-thirds of these unaffiliated adults still believe in God, pushing the total number of believers to ninety-one percent. See "'Nones' on the Rise," Pew Research Religion and Public Life Project, Oct. 9, 2012, www.pew forum.org/2012/10/09/nones-on-the-rise.

[2]Richard Swinburne, *Is There a God?* rev. ed. (New York: Oxford University Press), p. 40.

[3]Peter Kreeft and Ronald Tacelli, *Handbook of Christian Apologetics* (Downers Grove, IL: InterVarsity Press, 1994), p. 51.

[4]"The nothing before the big bang . . . is not a subject that can have properties, but is rather the absence of all properties." Douglas Groothuis, *Christian Apologetics: A Comprehensive Case for Biblical Faith* (Downers Grove, IL: IVP Academic, 2011), Kindle ed., chap. 11.

[5]Lee Strobel, *The Case for a Creator: A Journalist Investigates Scientific Evidence That Points Toward God* (Grand Rapids, MI: Zondervan, 2005), Kindle ed., chap. 11.

[6]Echoed by Richard Dawkins: "The designer hypothesis immediately raises the larger problem of who designed the designer." *The God Delusion* (Boston: Mariner, 2008), p. 145.

[7]William Lane Craig, "Dawkins's Delusion," in *Contending with Christianity's Critics: Answering New Atheists and Other Objectors*, ed. Paul Copan and William Lane Craig (Nashville: B&H Academic, 2009), Kindle ed., chap. 1.

[8]Christian philosophers speak of God as being "self-existent," meaning he does not depend on anything outside himself for his existence. C. Stephen Evans and R. Zachary Manis, *Philosophy of Religion: Thinking About Faith*, 2nd ed. (Downers Grove, IL: IVP Academic, 2009), p. 39.

[9]For example, the particular characteristics of matter/energy at the time of the Big Bang.

[10]Richard Swinburne, "Arguments to God from the Observable Uni-

verse," in *The Blackwell Companion to Science and Christianity,* ed. J. B. Stump and Alan G. Padgett (West Sussex, UK: Wiley-Blackwell, 2012), p. 123.

CHAPTER 4: THE WORLD IS LIKE A ROYAL FLUSH

[1]Antony Flew and Roy Abraham Varghese, *There Is a God: How the World's Most Notorious Atheist Changed His Mind* (New York: HarperOne, 2007), p. 93.

[2]Ibid., p. 88.

[3]The design argument is sometimes called the "teleological argument," from the Greek *teleios*—having to do with purpose and final ends.

[4]The fine-tuning argument is sometimes called the "anthropic principle."

[5]Robin Collins, "The Fine-Tuning of the Cosmos: A Fresh Look at Its Implications," in *The Blackwell Companion to Science and Christianity,* ed. J. B. Stump and Alan G. Padgett (West Sussex, UK: Wiley-Blackwell, 2012), p. 207.

[6]Robin Collins, "A Scientific Argument for the Existence of God: The Fine-Tuning Design Argument," in *Reason for the Hope Within,* ed. Michael J. Murray (Grand Rapids: Eerdmans, 1993), Kindle ed., chap. 3.

[7]John Jefferson Davis, *The Frontiers of Science and Faith: Examining Questions from the Big Bang to the End of the Universe* (Downers Grove, IL: InterVarsity Press, 2002), p. 132.

[8]Hugh Ross, "Big Bang Model Refined by Fire," in *Mere Creation,* ed. William A. Dembski (Downers Grove, IL: InterVarsity Press, 1998), pp. 372-80. See also a list of thirty-five parameters in Ross's *The Creator and the Cosmos: How the Greatest Scientific Discoveries of the Century Reveal God,* 3rd ed. (Colorado Springs, CO: NavPress, 2011), chap. 14.

[9]Robin Collins, "The Teleological Argument: An Exploration of the Fine-Tuning of the Universe," in *The Blackwell Companion to Natural Theology,* ed. William Lane Craig and J. P. Moreland (New York: Wiley, 2009), pp. 202-81.

[10]The cosmological constant, the strong and electromagnetic forces, carbon production in stars, the proton/neutron difference, the weak force and gravity.

[11]Alvin Plantinga, *Where the Conflict Really Lies: Science, Religion, and Naturalism* (New York: Oxford University Press, 2011), Kindle ed., chap. 7.

[12]Collins, "A Scientific Argument," chap. 3.

[13]Flew and Varghese, *There Is a God*, p. 114.

[14]Dr. David Clark of Bethel University first suggested the royal flush analogy to me.

[15]According to About.com guide Courtney Taylor, the probability of being dealt a royal flush is 0.00015 percent, or 1:649,740. "If you were dealt 20 hands of poker every night of the year, in 89 years you should only expect to see one royal flush." "What Is the Probability of Being Dealt a Royal Flush?" About.com Statistics, statistics.about.com/od/Applications/a/What-Is-The-Probability-Of-Being-Dealt-A-Royal-Flush.htm.

[16]It should be noted that there is also a specific intelligent design (ID) movement that focuses on information theory and usually stops short of specifying the exact nature of the designer. I'm using the phrase "intelligent design" in a broader sense, referring to arguments from design in general.

[17]C. Stephen Evans and R. Zachary Manis, *Philosophy of Religion: Thinking About Faith* (Downers Grove, IL: IVP Academic, 2009), p. 80.

[18]William Paley, *Natural Theology* (Oxford: Oxford University Press, 2008), p. 8.

[19]Richard Swinburne: "It is then immensely improbable that we should live in a multiverse that has the characteristic of producing at some stage a universe with laws and initial conditions like ours, when almost all possible multiverses would not produce such a universe." *The Blackwell Companion to Science and Christianity*, ed. J. B. Stump and Alan G. Padgett (West Sussex, UK: Wiley-Blackwell, 2012), p. 127.

[20]That is, concerned with larger questions of existence and knowledge.

[21]Victor Stenger, "Is the Universe Fine-Tuned for Us?" in *Why Intelligent Design Fails: A Scientific Critique of the New Creationism*, ed. Matt Young and Taner Edis (New Brunswick, NJ: Rutgers University Press, 2004), p. 184.

[22]The authors argue that many times whether a person accepts an argument or not is based on subjective factors such as "gut feel," or the "ring of truth." This should remind us to be genuinely respectful and caring toward our dialogue partners in presenting the Christian worldview. Evans and Manis, *Philosophy of Religion*, pp. 186-87.

[23]Flew and Varghese, *There Is a God*, p. 75.

[24]William Grimes, "Antony Flew, Philosopher and Ex-Atheist, Dies at 87," *The New York Times,* April 16, 2010, www.nytimes.com/2010/04/17 /arts/17flew.html.

CHAPTER 5: JESUS AS THE SON OF GOD

[1]Paul Rhodes Eddy and Gregory A. Boyd, *The Jesus Legend: A Case for the Historical Reliability of the Synoptic Jesus Tradition* (Grand Rapids, MI: Baker Academic, 2007), pp. 91-132.

[2]Ibid., p. 110.

[3]Hugh Bowden, *Mystery Cults of the Ancient World* (Princeton, NJ: Princeton University Press, 2010), p. 24.

[4]Luke Timothy Johnson, "Learning the Human Jesus," in *The Historical Jesus: Five Views* (Downers Grove, IL: InterVarsity Press, 2009), Kindle ed., chap. 3.

[5]Note that it is common among New Testament scholars to assign a certain level of interdependence among the Gospel writers, though not completely so. Thus Matthew and Luke probably used Mark's Gospel in oral or possibly written form, another probable source called Q (if real, it bolsters the case for the reliability of Matthew and Luke because it dates nearer to the time of Christ), plus their own independent material. John's familiarity with and dependence on the other Gospels is debated. The important point to note is that there is *partial* interdependence but also a level of independence in the four Gospels. See Arthur Patzia, *The Making of the New Testament,* 2nd ed. (Downers Grove, IL: InterVarsity Press, 2011), pp. 72-77.

[6]Craig L. Blomberg, *The Historical Reliability of the Gospels* (Downers Grove, IL: InterVarsity Press, 2007), p. 34.

[7]Eddy and Boyd, *Jesus Legend,* p. 409.

[8]Blomberg also notes that "despite two centuries of skeptical onslaught, it is fair to say that all the alleged inconsistencies among the Gospels have received at least plausible resolutions." *Historical Reliability,* pp. 35-36.

[9]Some Christians may wonder how the discrepancies in the Gospels fit with the idea of the inspiration of Scripture. In my view, ultimately there will be no direct contradictions. But we may never know the solutions to certain Gospel problems until the life to come. (See Robert H. Stein, *Difficult Passages in the New Testament: Interpreting Puzzling Texts in the*

Gospels and Epistles [Grand Rapids: Baker, 1990], p. 50.) The small claim here is that certain levels of "difference" among four accounts of the same events gives the ring of authenticity.

[10]For a helpful summary, see Eddy and Boyd, *Jesus Legend*, pp. 170-99.

[11]Henry Bettenson, *Documents of the Christian Church*, 2nd ed. (Oxford: Oxford University Press, 1967), p. 2.

[12]Flavius Josephus, *The Antiquities of the Jews* 20.9.1, in *Josephus: The Complete Works*, trans. William Whiston (BN Publishing, 2010).

CHAPTER 6: THE TELEPHONE GAME

[1]At Sonoma State in California: Why did Lucifer rebel against God? "I have no idea." At Case Western Reserve University in Cleveland: What happened to the dinosaurs? "Mmm, I should know that one, sorry." At South Texas College in McAllen: Can you interpret this dream I had last night? "Oh my goodness! Probably not . . . "

[2]Bart D. Ehrman, *Misquoting Jesus* (New York: HarperOne, 2009), Kindle ed., introduction.

[3]Dates are approximate. For Josephus, see Lee Strobel, *The Case for Christ* (Grand Rapids, MI: Zondervan, 1998), p. 60 (Bruce Metzger notes in his interview with Strobel that there is also a Latin copy of Josephus's *Jewish Wars* dated from the fourth century); for Homer, see Paul Rhodes Eddy and Gregory A. Boyd, *The Jesus Legend: A Case for the Historical Reliability of the Synoptic Jesus Tradition* (Grand Rapids, MI: Baker Academic, 2007), p. 383, citing Metzger; for Plato, see T. H. Irwin, "The Platonic Corpus," in *Oxford Handbook of Plato,* ed. Gail Fine (New York: Oxford University Press, 2008), p. 71.

[4]Craig L. Blomberg, "Jesus of Nazareth: How Historians Can Know Him and Why It Matters," in Douglas Groothuis, *Christian Apologetics: A Comprehensive Case for Biblical Faith* (Downers Grove, IL: IVP Academic, 2011), Kindle ed., chap. 19.

[5]Ibid.

[6]Ehrman, *Misquoting Jesus*, introduction.

[7]Blomberg, "Jesus of Nazareth," chap. 19.

[8]Ehrman, *Misquoting Jesus*, chap. 3.

[9]Craig L. Blomberg, *The Historical Reliability of the Gospels* (Downers Grove, IL: IVP Academic, 2007), p. 232.

[10]Timothy Paul Jones, *Misquoting Truth: A Guide to the Fallacies of Bart Ehrman's* Misquoting Jesus (Downers Grove, IL: InterVarsity Press, 2007), p. 44.

[11]Ibid., pp. 43-54.

[12]Ibid., p. 54.

CHAPTER 7: BROKEN WORLD

[1]Cornelius Plantinga Jr., "Sin: Not the Way It's Supposed to Be," Christ on Campus Initiative, 2010, henrycenter.tiu.edu/resource/sin-not-the-way-its-supposed-to-be/. See also Plantinga's full-length treatment of the topic in *Not the Way It's Supposed to Be: A Breviary of Sin* (Grand Rapids, MI: Eerdmans, 1995).

[2]Philosophers sometimes call this "libertarian" free will—that is, the freedom to make real choices that are not forced by God. So my choice to eat a bagel for breakfast this morning was "free" in the sense that I could have chosen to eat oatmeal instead, with no divine coercion either way.

[3]I'm speaking here to readers who hold a compatibilist view of God's sovereignty and human free will, which is usually Calvinist in its outlook.

[4]Paul Helm, "The Augustinian-Calvinist View," in *Divine Foreknowledge: Four Views*, ed. James K. Beilby and Paul R. Eddy (Downers Grove, IL: IVP Academic, 2001), p. 176.

CHAPTER 8: CHRISTIANS BEHAVING BADLY

[1]Note that Dunant was often critical of the church and lived a troubled life.

[2]See Alvin J. Schmidt, *How Christianity Changed the World* (Grand Rapids, MI: Zondervan, 2009), pp. 151-69.

[3]See David S. Dockery, "Integrating Faith and Learning in Higher Education," The Research Institute of the Ethics and Religious Liberty Commission, Council for Christian Colleges and Universities, Sept. 20, 2000, www.cccu.org/professional_development/resource_library/2004/integrating_faith__learning_in_higher_education.

[4]See W. C. Ringenberg, "Harvard University," "Yale University" and "Princeton University," in *Dictionary of Christianity in America*, ed. Daniel G. Reid et al. (Downers Grove, IL: InterVarsity Press, 1990), pp. 511, 1297, 942-43.

[5]"Yale, a Short History: The Making of the University," Yale University Library, www.library.yale.edu/mssa/YHO/Piersons/makingOfUniversity.html.

[6]A good starting point for many of these issues is Schmidt, *How Christianity Changed the World*.

[7]Jeffrey Burton Russell, *Exposing Myths About Christianity: A Guide to Answering 145 Viral Lies and Legends* (Downers Grove, IL: IVP Books, 2012), Kindle ed., chap. 14.

[8]Ibid., chap. 13.

CHAPTER 9: RELIGIONS ARE LIKE BOOKS

[1]Stephen Prothero, *God Is Not One: The Eight Rival Religions That Run the World—and Why Their Differences Matter* (New York: HarperCollins, 2010), Kindle ed., introduction.

[2]See Prothero's helpful discussion of religious differences in *God Is Not One*, introduction and conclusion.

[3]Timothy Keller, *The Reason for God* (New York: Dutton, 2008), p. 19.

CHAPTER 10: CAN THOSE WHO'VE NEVER HEARD OF JESUS BE SAVED?

[1]Gregory Boyd, *Letters from a Skeptic* (Wheaton, IL: Victor Books, 1994), p. 125.

[2]As opposed to "special revelation," which refers to God revealing himself in the person of Christ and the Scriptures.

[3]Peter Kreeft and Ronald Tacelli, *Handbook of Christian Apologetics* (Downers Grove, IL: InterVarsity Press, 1994), p. 327.

[4]For summary discussions on prevenient grace, see Alister E. McGrath, *Christian Theology: An Introduction* (Malden, MA: Blackwell, 2001), pp. 449-51; Millard J. Erickson, *Christian Theology* (Grand Rapids, MI: Baker, 1995), pp. 914-31.

[5]Kreeft and Tacelli, *Handbook*, pp. 327-28.

[6]David Clark, "Religious Pluralism and Christian Exclusivism," in *To Everyone an Answer: A Case for the Christian Worldview* (Downers Grove, IL: InterVarsity Press, 2004), pp. 299-300.

[7]Ibid.

CHAPTER 11: HELL IS LIKE AN EMPTY PUB

[1]For a helpful overview of four different theological positions on hell, see

Four Views on Hell, ed. William Crockett (Grand Rapids, MI: Zondervan, 1996).

[2]The empty pub image assumes a "free-will" understanding of heaven and hell. A vast majority of the Christian students I encounter in my travels to secular colleges and universities hold to this view, so I am focusing my efforts there in the interest of serving them.

[3]While Scripture does not use the word *Trinity* per se, the concept is developed in a variety of passages such as Mark 1:9-11; John 14:25-26 and John 17:20-23.

[4]See C. S. Lewis, "The Trouble with 'X,'" in *God in the Dock: Essays on Theology and Ethics* (Grand Rapids: Eerdmans, 1970), part 1, chap. 18; also, *The Problem of Pain* (New York: Macmillan, 1962), chap. 8, esp. p. 128.

[5]James Joyce, *The Portable James Joyce* (New York: Viking, 1966), pp. 371-74.

[6]Quoted in Stanley Hauerwas and William Willimon, *Resident Aliens* (Nashville: Abingdon Press, 1989), p. 33.

[7]Michael J. Murray, "The Literal View," in *Reason for the Hope Within*, ed. Michael J. Murray (Grand Rapids, MI: Eerdmans, 1999), Kindle ed., chap. 12.

[8]John Walvoord, "Heaven and Hell," in *Four Views on Hell*, Kindle ed., chap. 1.

[9]Gregory Boyd, *Letters from a Skeptic* (Wheaton, IL: Victor Books, 1994), p. 163.

[10]This is not an exhaustive list: see also Matthew 5:22, 29-30; 7:23; 18:9; 22:13; 23:15, 33; 25:29-30, 41; Mark 9:43-48; Luke 12:5; 1 Thessalonians 5:3, 9; 2 Thessalonians 1:8-9; Hebrews 6:8; 10:27; 2 Peter 2:4, 9; Revelation 1:18; 6:8; 20:10, 12-15; 21:8.

CHAPTER 12: ELEPHANT TRAPS

[1]Thomas Nagel, "A Philosopher Defends Religion," *The New York Review of Books*, Sept. 27, 2012, www.nybooks.com/articles/archives/2012/sep/27/philosopher-defends-religion.

[2]Richard Dawkins, *The God Delusion* (Boston: Mariner, 2008), p. 63.

[3]Natalie Wolchover, "Will Science Someday Rule Out the Possibility of God"? Science on NBC News.com, Sept. 18, 2012, www.nbcnews.com/id/49074598/ns/technology_and_science-science/t/will-science-someday-rule-out-possibility-god/.

CHAPTER 13: MIRACLES ARE LIKE A HOLE IN ONE

[1]Jennifer Gregory, "What Are the Odds of Hitting a Hole in One?" Golf Link, www.golflink.com/facts_8065_what-odds-hitting-hole-one.html.
[2]See Hume's case against miracles in section ten, "Of Miracles," in David Hume, *An Enquiry Concerning Human Understanding*.
[3]C. S. Lewis, *God in the Dock: Essays on Theology and Ethics* (Grand Rapids: Eerdmans, 1970), Kindle ed., part 1, chap. 2.

CHAPTER 14: HOW TO TALK WITH SKEPTICS

[1]Don Everts and Doug Schaupp, *I Once Was Lost: What Postmodern Skeptics Taught Us About Their Path to Jesus* (Downers Grove, IL: InterVarsity Press, 2008), pp. 29-48.
[2]Adam S. McHugh, *Introverts in the Church: Finding Our Place in an Extroverted Culture* (Downers Grove, IL: InterVarsity Press, 2009), Kindle ed., chap. 5.
[3]See ibid., chap. 8, for how introverted Christians can reach out in ways that are natural to their temperament while still assuming appropriate risk.
[4]For suggestions on how to pray for non-Christians, see Rick Richardson, *Reimagining Evangelism* (Downers Grove, IL: InterVarsity Press, 2006), pp. 43-45.
[5]It should be noted that most folks come down somewhere on a spectrum between modern and postmodern and thus exhibit traits of both. Still, I think it's useful to discern which way they lean.
[6]For a short comparison of modernism and postmodernism, see Chris Sinkinson, *Christian Confidence: An Introduction to Defending the Faith* (Downers Grove, IL: InterVarsity Press, 2012), pp. 109-22.
[7]For a more extensive treatment of postmodernism, see Stanley J. Grenz, *A Primer on Postmodernism* (Grand Rapids, MI: Eerdmans, 1996).

CHAPTER 15: HOW TO TALK WITH MODERN SKEPTICS WHO BELIEVE IN GOD

[1]Barry A. Kosmin and Juhem Navarro-Rivera, "The Transformation of Generation X: Shifts in Religious and Political Self-Identification, 1990-2008," Trinity College, commons.trincoll.edu/aris/files/2012/05/ARISGENX2012.pdf; "The Generation Gap and the 2012 Election," Pew Research Center for the People and the Press, Nov. 3, 2011, www.people-press.org/2011/11/03/section-1-how-generations-have-changed.

CHAPTER 16: HOW TO TALK WITH MODERN ATHEISTS

[1]To help counter an anti-intellectual mindset in the church, see J. P. Moreland, *Love Your God with All Your Mind* (Colorado Springs, CO: NavPress, 1997); and David A. Horner, *Mind Your Faith* (Downers Grove, IL: InterVarsity Press, 2011).

[2]Alister McGrath and Joanna Collicutt McGrath, *The Dawkins Delusion? Atheist Fundamentalism and the Denial of the Divine* (Downers Grove, IL: IVP Books, 2007), p. 11.

[3]Alvin Plantinga, *Where the Conflict Really Lies: Science, Religion, and Naturalism* (New York: Oxford University Press, 2011), Kindle ed., preface.

[4]This is what theologian James Beilby refers to as "deconstructive apologetics." This means you're trying to show not just the attractiveness of Christianity but the deficiency of other views, in this case atheism. See Beilby, *Thinking About Christian Apologetics* (Downers Grove, IL: IVP Academic, 2011), p. 15.

[5]For models of how to engage in deconstructive apologetics, see J. P. Moreland's interactions with atheist Kai Nielsen in *Does God Exist? The Great Debate* (Nashville: Thomas Nelson, 1990); also the YouTube recording of William Lane Craig debating Sam Harris at the University of Notre Dame, "The God Debate II: Harris vs. Craig," YouTube, April 12, 2011, www.youtube.com/watch?v=yqaHXKLRKzg, in which Craig spends considerable time trying to show the flaws in Harris's views rather than exclusively defending Christianity.

[6]C. Stephen Evans and R. Zachary Manis, *Philosophy of Religion: Thinking About Faith* (Downers Grove, IL: IVP Academic, 2009), p. 32.

[7]Ibid., pp. 52-54.

[8]Tom was particularly influenced by Lee Strobel's *The Case for Christ* (Grand Rapids, MI: Zondervan, 1998), and N. T. Wright's *The Meaning of Jesus: Two Visions* (New York: HarperCollins, 1999), coauthored with Marcus Borg.

CHAPTER 17: HOW TO TALK WITH POSTMODERN SEEKERS AND SKEPTICS

[1]Rick Richardson, *Reimagining Evangelism* (Downers Grove, IL: InterVarsity Press, 2006), p. 37.

[2]Don Everts and Doug Schaupp, *I Once Was Lost: What Postmodern*

Skeptics Taught Us About Their Path to Jesus (Downers Grove, IL: Inter-Varsity Press, 2008), pp. 23-24.

[3]For an extended treatment of soul-awakening events, see Rick Richardson, *Evangelism Outside the Box* (Downers Grove, IL: InterVarsity Press, 2000), pp. 80-91, 183-86. Richardson gives a general theory of soul awakening that includes tapping into non-Christians' felt needs, establishing common ground and linking their deepest longings to the gospel. Paul's interactions with the Athenian philosophers in Acts 17 is his model.

[4]Erik Brandt's music can be found at www.urbanhillbillyquartet.com. Quite intentionally, many of his songs have Christian undertones while not being overtly Christian. He feels comfortable in postmodern culture.

[5]Note that there are numerous academic treatments to help us understand postmodernism and its adherents. Three examples are David K. Clark, *To Know and Love God* (Wheaton, IL: Crossway, 2003), pp. 99-132; James Sire, *The Universe Next Door*, 3rd ed. (Downers Grove, IL: InterVarsity Press 1997), pp. 172-91; and Stanley Grenz, *A Primer on Postmodernism* (Grand Rapids, MI: Eerdmans, 1996).

[6]This is sometimes called "self-referentially incoherent." It means that a statement doesn't pass its own test. Thus the statement "Relativism is true" is incoherent, because in relativism there is no final truth. But if it's true that there is no final truth, then relativism can't be true either. It's like saying, "Everything I say is a lie." But of course I'm also lying when I say that. Again, incoherent.

[7]Mark Miller, *Experiential Storytelling: (Re)Discovering Narrative to Communicate God's Message* (Grand Rapids, MI: Zondervan, 2003); Christine Dillon, *Telling the Gospel Through Story: Evangelism That Keeps Hearers Wanting More* (Downers Grove, IL: IVP Books, 2012).

[8]For two representative books on the postmodern inclination to reject organized religion while remaining open to Jesus, see Rick James, *Jesus Without Religion* (Downers Grove, IL: IVP Books, 2007); and Dan Kimball, *They Like Jesus but Not the Church* (Grand Rapids, MI: Zondervan, 2007).

[9]Everts and Schaupp, *I Once Was Lost*, pp. 60-61.

[10]The remarkable story can be read in his autobiography, Ahmed Ali Haile and David W. Shenk, *Teatime in Mogadishu: My Journey as a Peace Ambassador in the World of Islam* (Harrisonburg, VA: Herald, 2011).

[11]Though the white robe and book of life were actual physical props, we were careful to explain them as symbols only.

EPILOGUE

[1]James Sire, *Why Good Arguments Often Fail* (Downers Grove, IL: IVP Books, 2006), pp. 182-83.

Index

apologetics, 28-35
    balanced with reliance
        on Holy Spirit, 190-91,
        213-14
    deconstructive, 225
    definition of, 13
    purpose of, 114
    suggested resources, 178
    See also cumulative case
atheism
    critique by Lee Strobel,
        40
    as a grand story, 208
    and hypocrisy, 107-9
    and naturalism, 37
    the new, 187-88
    presumption of, 146-47
Barton, Clara, 104
Beilby, James, 31, 225
Bowden, Hugh, 63
beneficial order, 52-57, 154
big bang, 39-44, 48, 189, 216
Blomberg, Craig, 66, 78-79
Boyd, Gregory, 124
Clark, David K., 130-31, 196,
    218
Christian community, 17, 18,
    24, 101, 135-36, 140, 157,
    175, 183, 191, 202, 209-10
Collins, Robin, 48-51
conversation skills and
    strategies
    in dialogue with an
        atheist, 155-58
    dysfunctional family
        analogy for
        non-philosophers,
        89-90
    handling rejection, 42
    in judging salvation,
        123-24
    regarding design, 53-57
    regarding faith and
        evidence, 22-24
    regarding fine-tuning,
        49-50
    regarding hell, 137-40
    regarding hypocrisy,
        98-109
    regarding miracles, 160,
        164-67

regarding religious
    pluralism, 111-14,
    120-21
regarding science
    detecting God, 147-48
regarding testimony of
    the historical Jesus,
    70-72
in telling stories, 208
in telling the Big Story,
    92-93
using images, 12-14
using the cumulative
    case, 29-33
using the marriage
    analogy, 27
with a relativist, 206-7
with modernist atheists,
    186-95
with moderns, 180-84
with postmoderns,
    199-200, 206-8
with science-only
    skeptics, 147-50, 157
with seekers and
    skeptics in general,
    171-78
cosmology, 37-44, 148
    See also creation, infinite
    regress
creation
    and fall, 90
    brokenness, 84-87
    dominion, 98
    ex-nihilo, 37-38, 44
    exploring, 55-56, 151
    as general revelation, 125
    of gravity, 154
    of human beings, 86-87,
        94-95, 125, 136, 138,
        187
    like a novelist, 148-49
Craig, William Lane, 41
Crouch, Andy, 31
cumulative case, 29-35, 54,
    56, 186-87
Davis, John Jefferson, 48
Dawkins, Richard, 147, 152,
    187-88, 190
design/designer, 37-38, 43,
    44, 46-57, 147-48, 216, 217,

218.
    See also fine-tuning
divine serendipity, 126
dominion impulse, 98,
    100-101
Dunant, Henry, 104, 221
Eddy, Paul, 220
Ehrman, Bart, 77-82
epistemology, 208
evangelism
    and clarifying of
        conversion, 26
    community-based, 191
    and listening, 200
    modern, postmodern,
        177-78
    by a non-evangelist, 204
    and soul-awakening
        events, 226
    onion skin method of,
        171-73
    See also five thresholds
    of conversion
eternal universe, 39-40, 44
    See also cosmology
Evans, C. Stephen, 52, 57
Everts, Don, 174, 200-201,
    203, 210
evidence, 19-24, 27, 30-32,
    42, 46, 50, 54, 66, 69-71,
    78, 124, 126, 145-48, 153,
    156, 158, 161-62, 165-66,
    188-89, 195, 197, 215.
    See also cumulative case,
    faith
evil
    moral, 85-86, 94
    natural, 55, 85-86, 94
    problem of, 10, 31, 85,
        88-94
exclusivity
    of Christianity versus
        Islam, 116
    and cultural inclusivity,
        129
    of Jesus, Christianity, 98,
        117-21, 123, 129-30
faith
    blind, 77, 187, 194-95
    case for, 13, 31, 185, 187,
        213

evidential/rational,
   19-25, 27, 29, 47, 89
informed, 23, 25
lack of, 67, 84, 86, 123,
   181, 190
rational/emotional,
   17-19, 25-27, 29, 67
saving, 91, 126-30,
   196-97, 201-5, 211
and science, 146
   See also cumulative case,
      evidence, fideism
fall (of Genesis 3), 85-86,
   88-90, 94, 126, 131, 152
Ferrell, Will, 149
fideism, 20-21
fine-tuning, 47-57, 217
   See also design
five thresholds of conversion,
   200-205
   See also evangelism
Flew, Antony, 46-47, 51, 53,
   55, 57, 146-47
free will, 86-89, 93-95,
   137-39, 189, 221, 223
god-of-the-gaps, 55-56
Gospels, 23, 26, 61-75, 174,
   214
   conspiracy theories of,
      12, 72-75
   discrepancies in, 62,
      65-67, 74
   embarrassing material
      in, 62, 67-68
   and hell, 137
   manuscripts of, 62, 68,
      75, 77-82
   and multiple attestation,
      70
   overlapping material in,
      64-65
   and secular sources, 62,
      68-72, 75
   and stewarding
      resources, 130
   studying the, 183, 205,
      209
   variants in, 78-80
Groothuis, Douglas, 30, 216
Habitat for Humanity, 103,
   105, 109
Haile, Ahmed and Sofia,
   211-12, 226

hell, 55, 72, 84, 86, 134-40,
   180-82, 184, 188, 222-23
Hellenism, 62-64
Helm, Paul, 88
Hick, John, 114-16
Holy Spirit, 12, 42, 72, 87,
   90, 172, 174, 176, 186,
   190-91, 194, 213-14
Homer, 77
Hume, David, 160-67
hypocrisy, 11, 33, 97-109,
   209
infinite regress, 39-40, 44
   See also cosmology
Johnson, Luke Timothy, 64
Jones, Timothy Paul, 79,
   81-82
Josephus, Flavius, 71, 75, 77,
   220
Keller, Timothy, 119, 178
Kreeft, Peter, 39, 125, 128
LeBlanc, Terry, 100
Lewis, C. S., 10, 29, 61, 137,
   164
Manis, Zachary, 52, 57
McGrath, Alister, 222
   and Joanna Collicut, 188
McHugh, Adam, 175
miracles, 67, 75, 91, 149, 155,
   159-67
modernism, 12, 146-47, 173,
   176-95, 200, 208
monotheism, 62-63, 74
mystery religions, 62-64
multiverse, 54
Murray, Michael, 139
Nagel, Thomas, 146, 188
naturalism, 37, 40, 150, 189
   See also atheism
Nightingale, Florence, 104
nones (the), 216
objective truth, 187, 208
Occam's razor. *See*
   parsimony
Paley, William, 52-53
parsimony, 152-55, 158
philosophy, 28, 89, 108, 110,
   153
   as pointing to God,
      29-30, 34, 54
   and science, 41-42,
      150-51, 158
Plantinga, Alvin, 51, 54, 188

Plantinga, Cornelius, 85, 221
Plato, 77-78
postmodernism, 12, 110,
   173, 176-79, 184, 199-212,
   226
prayer, 12, 24, 33, 42, 84-91,
   94, 102, 119, 131, 172-74,
   176, 183, 186-87, 189,
   195-97, 201-5, 210-211,
   224
prevenient grace, 125-26,
   131, 222
proof, 17, 21-22, 27, 46, 70,
   76, 124-25, 145-47, 155-57,
   166, 193-94
Prothero, Stephen, 111
Red Cross, 103-4
relativism, 206, 226
religious pluralism, 31,
   110-21, 123, 129, 199-200
revelation
   book of, 211
   general, 115, 124-30
   special, 222
Richardson, Rick, 200-201,
   224, 226
Ross, Hugh, 48-50
Rowling, J. K., 149
Russell, Jeffrey Burton, 106
Sagan, Carl, 150
Schaupp, Doug, 174,
   200-201, 203, 210
science, 24, 46, 187, 196
   authority of, 118, 182
   and the big bang, 40-42
   and certitude, 27
   and fine-tuning, 47-50
   and god-of-the-gaps,
      55-56
   historical, 56
   as an indicator of God,
      29, 34, 47, 54, 147-48
   limitations of, 148,
      156-58
   misuse of, 106-7, 109
   of-the-gaps, 54-55
   and an open universe,
      148-51, 158
   and philosophy, 40-42,
      56, 150-51, 155-56,
      158, 160, 195
   as a supposed
      comprehensive

explanation of the
  universe, 56, 151-52,
  158, 166, 183-84
as the supposed simplest
  explanation of the
  universe, 152-55, 158
testability of, 56
versus faith/subjectivity,
  22, 32-33, 145-47, 158,
  163-65, 195
versus humanities, 177
self-referentially incoherent,
  226
Sire, James, 28-29, 195,

213-14
soul-awakening events,
  201-2, 226
Stalin, Joseph, 107-8
Stinger, Victor, 56
storytelling, 207-9
Strobel, Lee, 40, 197, 220
Swinburne, Richard, 38, 42,
  44, 218
Tacelli, Ronald, 39, 125,
  128
Tacitus, 70-71, 75
Thucydides, 77-78
Trinity, 21, 33, 136, 223

Varghese, Roy Abraham, 47,
  51
Walvoord, John, 139
Wilberforce, William, 106
worldview, 18, 20, 28
  atheistic, 163-64, 167
  definition of, 37
  faults of, 105, 107
  as neighboring tribes,
    190
  presenting the Christian,
    22
  scientific, 195